BIGGLES ON

'There was no reason why this man should die here.'

'No reason at all. I'd say he was killed by the creatures that devoured him.'

'What about the dogs?' said Ginger. 'We were told there were dogs here.'

'Biggles nodded. 'I was waiting for someone to say that. It begins to look as if there might be something in the story after all.'

Hardly had the words left his lips than from somewhere in the jungle came a low, ferocious growl.

About the author

Captain W. E. Johns, who died in 1968 at age of 75, served with considerable distinction in the R.F.C. in World War 1. After working with the R.A.F. in peacetime he became a prominent Air Correspondent and author of aviation books, and in 1932 he founded the magazine *Popular Flying*. Biggles first appeared in short stories in the same year, a character who was typical of the kind of man Captain Johns knew in the War.

Altogether Captain Johns wrote 85 books about Biggles, who has now become one of the most famous characters in children's fiction.

Biggles on Mystery Island

Captain W. E. Johns

KNIGHT BOOKS
Hodder and Stoughton

First published in 1958 by Hodder and Stoughton Ltd.

Knight Books edition 1984

British Library C.I.P.

Johns, W.E.
Biggles on mystery island.—(Knight books)
I. Title
823'.912[J] PZ7

ISBN 0 340 34838 0

The characters and situations in this book are entirely imaginary and bear no relation to any real person or actual happening.

Printed and bound in Great Britain for Hodder and Stoughton Paperbacks, a division of Hodder and Stoughton Ltd., Mill Road, Dunton Green, Sevenoaks, Kent (Editorial Office: 47 Bedford Square, London, WC1 3DP) by Hunt Barnard Printing Ltd., Aylesbury, Bucks.

CONTENTS

Chapter 1

OBJECTIVE PACIFIC

The four 'Pegasus' engines that powered the old converted Sunderland flying-boat, on the strength of the Special Air Police Flight for remote marine operations, kicked the air behind them with a steady, deep-throated roar that might have been a challenge to anyone who dared to suggest that age had impaired their efficiency. With effortless ease they bore the big aircraft on a course north-east under a sky that would have been empty had it not been for two small thunderstorms which, far to the west, were apparently engaged in a trans-Pacific cloud-race.

For the rest of the sky was a clear, uniform turquoise. Below and around, the vast circle of horizon that ringed the edge of the world would also have been unbroken but for a fast-fading smudge, dead astern, that marked the towering peak of Nuku Hiva, largest of the group of eleven islands known as the Marquesas.

Six men occupied seats in the one-time military machine, either at the controls or lounging in the cabin. They were Biggles, his three staff pilots Algy, Bertie and Ginger, Marcel Brissac of the French Sécurité Nationale, and a Swedish police officer named Sven Heldersen, whose presence in the party will be explained presently.

Marcel was there for two main reasons. Firstly, to

facilitate the passage of the Sunderland through the many Pacific islands known as French Polynesia, where it might have to land, and secondly, because, as will be seen, France had an interest in the investigation on which the Sunderland was engaged; for, while the ultimate objective was Oratovoa, a British possession, the island raised its rocky mass from the sea close enough to the French Marquesas to be called a neighbour. The actual distance from where it lay, just below the Equator, to the nearest of the Marquesas, was three hundred miles, but this, as distances are reckoned in the Pacific, was like being next door.

The Sunderland was now on the last leg of its long flight from England, its course, governed by its endurance range, having been via Australia, Fiji and Tahiti, capital of French Polynesia, and finally Atuona, on the island of Hiva-oa, one of the Marquesas. The purpose of this last call was to make enquiries, and to check certain information. Marcel had gone to see the French Resident agent while Biggles had paid a visit to an old acquaintance, a Chinese storekeeper named Ah Song.

The trip, at a comfortable cruising speed, for there was no urgency – as far as they were aware – about the operation, had occupied a period of just under six weeks.

The purpose of the aircraft in such remote waters can soon be narrated. The business had begun with an exchange of notes between the Colonial Offices of Britain and France. Later, there had been a general enquiry from Sweden in respect of missing persons, this having been instigated at the request of relatives.

What the fuss was really about nobody seemed to

know. And it may well have been, in the early stages at all events, nobody cared. It was all vague and very much in the air, and as government offices do not look for trouble the file on the case was pushed around in the hope, no doubt, that it would be forgotten.

The only information that might be called definite had come, as was to be expected considering the French possessions in the region, from Tahiti, administrative centre of French Polynesia, originally known to the world as the South Sea Islands. Even so, Tahiti knew little enough. All it could say was that over the past eighteen months two traders, one a Polynesian and the other French, had sailed for Oratovoa and neither had returned. In both cases the vessels were old, and small, and of no particular consequence to anyone except their owner-captains. The crews were Polynesians. But it happened that the French boat had carried as passenger a Catholic missionary, a volunteer who had gone out to explore new ground, and his bishop wanted to know what had become of him.

There was of course no proof that either ship had reached its destination. On the other hand there was no reason why they should not have done so. At the time the weather had been fine. Both had called at the Marquesas, where some business had been conducted. They were all right then. Both were to have called on their way back to Tahiti, but there had been no news of them since. This, naturally, had led to some speculation about their fates, but nothing was done, and the mystery was half forgotten when it was revived by the disappearance of another vessel.

A small private yacht named *Dryad*, owned by a

Dutchman, which had been cruising among the islands filming for a television series, had last been seen heading for Oratovoa. It had called at Hiva-oa, in the Marquesas, for stores, some of which were to be picked up later. In the meantime the Dutch owner-skipper declared his intention of shooting some film on Oratovoa. Nothing had since been seen of the yacht. It had not picked up its stores. It had not returned to Tahiti. There were two women on board, the owner's wife and daughter. Also on board was a Polynesian pilot of island experience.

What had happened to the *Dryad*? There had been no hurricane. Was its disappearance in connection with Oratovoa merely a coincidence? Nobody knew. However, apparently the French government decided it was time something was done. It sent a naval frigate to have a look round. It sailed slowly round the island but could see no sign of life. It stayed for two days. There was no sign of wreckage. Following this a British Naval Supply ship had been diverted by the Admiralty to have a look at the island in passing. The Captain made a report identical with that of the French commander. There was nobody there. Actually, this surprised no one, for Oratovoa had long been labelled 'uninhabited', for reasons which anyone knowing anything about the islands was well aware.

The main group of the Marquesas had within living memory carried a teeming population, reckoned to be in the order of a hundred and fifty thousand: but diseases introduced by European and Asian visitors, against which the Marquesans, who were Polynesians, had no inherent immunity, had played such havoc that the survivors were now numbered at not more than two thousand. Influenza alone wiped out tens of thousands between the wars. On some of the Marquesas not a soul remained alive, and it was thought that the same fate had befallen Oratovoa.

Apart from disease the nature of the island itself was of a sort hardly likely to encourage new settlers, as emerged from enquiries made by Biggles at the various government departments where such information, provided by mariners and explorers, is filed for reference.

Like all the Marquesas Oratovoa was volcanic in origin. At some unknown period in the past the island had in fact been a volcano which, before expiring to be classed as 'extinct', had blown out its centre, not only covering everything with dust and ashes, but causing the rock itself to become friable and therefore dangerous to move about on. This, it was thought, had happened long before European explorers had arrived on the scene, so that there were no longer visible signs of disaster. Since it lay near the Equator, and had a regular rainfall, nature had soon covered the scars with an almost inpenetrable cloak of tropical vegetation, that stretched from the sea well up towards the central summit.

This, and the size of the island, seemed to be the only physical features about which there was no doubt. According to Admiralty records the island was roughly oval in shape, seven miles long and four miles wide, rising sharply from the sea on all sides to a central summit nearly four thousand feet high – a formation common to most of the neighbouring Marquesas. Sailing Directions listed two anchorages where landings could be made almost at any time. One was a small bay sheltered by the island from the prevailing wind, and the other a narrow arm of the sea that cut deep into the land. Everywhere else the seas broke heavily all the year round, due to the absence of a reef on which the ocean rollers could trip and dash themselves to pieces. Navigation was made dangerous by rocks of all sizes that had fallen from the cliffs or had been cast from the island at the time of eruption.

The fact of the matter was, as Biggles was not slow to perceive when the Air Commodore first discussed the matter with him, nobody was really sure of anything. Nobody could be found who had been to the island in recent years, wherefore the information available, such as it was, could only be regarded with suspicion since it was out of date and anything could have happened in the meantime. The recent official surveys from the sea meant little. Ships could sail round the island, but because the crews saw no sign of human activity it did not mean nobody was there, particularly if the occupants, should there be any, did not wish to be seen. As for the mountainous centre of the island, it might have been part of the moon for all that was known of it. The only vehicle from which it could be surveyed was an aircraft.

Rumour is a strange thing. It is often impossible to trace the source, and no one can say where it will end. The only certain thing about it is, it loses nothing by repetition. Rumour flies as fast in the wide open spaces as it does in thickly populated areas of the earth's surface. No one could be found who could swear he had landed on Oratovoa, much less claim he had seen anyone there; yet rumours persisted, and on the principle that there was no smoke without fire it was felt in Whitehall that sooner or later steps would have to be taken to ascertain if there was any foundation for them. But no Department was anxious to accept responsibility for this, particularly as it was likely to prove an expensive business.

In due course the file on the case reached Air Commodore Raymond. He, like others who had read the papers, was not enthusiastic about 'carrying the bag', as Biggles put it, when the matter was brought to his notice. They discussed it at some length, and then it was Biggles himself who, by a casual remark, introduced an angle which apparently had not occurred to anyone. It was this new approach which landed him with the job of unravelling the tangle of Mystery Island, as Ginger dubbed the place when he was told about it. He claimed it was easier to remember that the island's proper name, and as this was obviously true, Mystery Island it became from that moment.

In discussing the matter with Biggles, the Air Commodore remarked that the days of taking things for granted were passing. Land grabbers were at work, and islands, even the most remote specks of land, were fast acquiring a new importance as military bases. For this the aeroplane, which could go anywhere, was largely responsible. National Defence, in a world unsettled by Power Politics, made it more than ever necessary for every nation to keep an eye on its property. This made clear the lines on which the Air Commodore was thinking.

Biggles was standing looking at the big wall map of

the Pacific.

'Well,' he replied, casually, 'all I can say is, if anyone has grabbed Oratovoa and thinks he's sitting pretty he may be fooling himself.'

'What do you mean?'

'He may get a shock before he's much older.'

'How so?'

'Oratovoa is within a thousand miles of Christmas Island, and you know what's going to happen there.'

'You mean, nuclear tests.'

'Yes.'

'A thousand miles is a long way.'

'If the radioactive fall-out of an American bomb could kill Japanese fishermen nearly five hundred miles away, I don't see why, should the wind happen to be blowing in the right direction, east-south-east, radioactivity shouldn't fall on Oratovoa. Should anyone be there it would be just too bad.'

Frowning, the Air Commodore rose from his desk and walked across the room to the map. 'Yes,' he muttered. 'You're right. I don't think anyone can have thought of that possibility.'

'If we happen to smother a lot of people, no matter who they may be, someone will have to do some hard thinking to find an excuse,' asserted Biggles, grimly. 'People all over the world are objecting to these nuclear tests and you can't blame them for that.'

For some seconds the Air Commodore did not answer. He lit a cigarette and drew on it thoughtfully. 'You're right,' he said at last. 'We shall have to do something about this.'

'Do what?'

'I'll report the risk to the Higher Authority right away.'

'They won't thank you for that.'

'Why not?'

'These atomic wizards would have to jam the brakes on their arrangements which are now far advanced. They wouldn't dare to go on after a warning from you. If they killed someone, and the story got into the Press, they wouldn't have a leg to stand on. The balloon would go up. Would they blame themselves? Not on your life! True, they might take the rap, but that would only make them more savage with you for pointing out the danger. You know how it is. If you send this file back to where it came from, with a warning, you'll be sticking your neck out.'

'What's the alternative? If I say nothing, and there is an accident, it would be on my conscience.'

'There wouldn't necessarily be an accident. That could only happen if there *were* people on Oratovoa. According to this file the island is uninhabited.'

'That's the official belief. But is it known for certain? According to local rumour something sinister is happening there. Nobody knows what. It seems to me, sir, that the first thing to do is confirm beyond any shadow of doubt that the rumours are bunk and that the island is in fact uninhabited. If there's no one there, okay. Let the tests go on. If there is somebody there he can be warned of what might happen. If, then, he decides to stay there, he will have only himself to blame should the sky start raining radioactive dust.'

'To get the information we want someone will have to go there.'

'Of course.'

'You realise who that will be?'

Biggles grinned. 'Me, I suppose. In stopping someone else from sticking his neck out I've now stuck my own out. I'm always doing that sort of thing. It's time I had more sense.'

'Well, what about it?'

Biggles shrugged. 'I don't mind going. It's time somebody went, anyway, if only to squash these rumours. If I'm to go I'd better get on with it.'

'There's plenty of time.'

'There may not be too much should it become necessary to evacuate a large group of inhabitants.'

'You think that could happen?'

'On a job like this anything could happen. Or perhaps nothing. I shall know more about that when I've been to Oratovoa.'

'Go and have a look,' decided the Air Commodore.

And that's how the matter was left.

Biggles' first step had been to fly to Paris to see Marcel Brissac and find out if he knew anything about Oratovoa, since it was no great distance from the French Marquesas. Marcel knew nothing. Indeed, he had never heard of the island. They looked at it on the map.

'There it is,' said Biggles, pointing at the speck. 'As you see, there are no regular shipping routes near it. It happens to lie in the centre of a triangle formed by the routes San Francisco-Tahiti, Panama-Honolulu and Salina Cruz to Tahiti.'

Marcel asked for a day or two to make enquiries at the French Colonial Bureau.

While he was waiting Biggles flew to Stockholm to go into the Swedish question about missing persons. There he had met, for the first time, Sven Heldersen, police liaison officer with Interpol. His story was fairly simple. It seemed that an advertisement had appeared in a Swedish newspaper offering to anyone dissatisfied with conditions in civilisation a new home on a South Sea Island. To this a number of people had replied. Four had actually accepted and gone. These were a young married couple and two students. Nothing had been heard of them since. The father of one of the students was a rich man and it was he who, naturally, wanted to know what had happened to his son.

He was able to provide some meagre information. His son had been asked to deposit five hundred pounds as a guarantee of good faith. This he had done, not so much because he wanted to escape from civilisation as to embark on what promised to be an adventure. The other student was a friend who went to keep him company. All these people had presumably invested five hundred pounds in the enterprise. Little more was known. They had boarded a small yacht in the harbour. Its destination was unknown, but was thought to be a British possession near the Marquesas. Even this was not certain. The boy's father had regarded the project with suspicion from the outset on account of the mystery surrounding it, but the boy, keen to go, had been allowed to have his way. There had been no mention of Oratovoa.

As in the case of Marcel, Sven Heldersen had never heard of the place. When he heard that Biggles intended flying out to it he expressed a wish to be allowed to join the party, if for no other reason than he would be able to identify the Swedish nationals, if they were found, and talk to them in their own language. As there was plenty of room no objection was raised, and that was how he came to be in the aircraft.

When Biggles got back to London he found Marcel there, waiting for him. His enquiries had produced one item of news, but this, far from casting any light on the affair, only served to deepen the mystery surrounding it. Briefly, it was this.

A canoe load of Polynesians from Taha-Uka, in the Marquesas, had been driven off their course by heavy weather. They had run to Oratovoa for shelter and water. Having landed, they were looking for water when they were attacked by a pack of mad dogs and had only saved themselves by rushing into the sea and swimming back to their canoe. They thought they had heard someone shouting at the dogs but they didn't see anyone. On reaching home they had reported the incident to the French resident official, who had in turn mentioned it in his routine report to Headquarters. Marcel had learned of the incident at the Colonial Office in Paris.

'Well, well,' murmured Biggles cynically. 'So now we have a pack of ravening hounds in the picture!'

'You don't believe it?'

'It doesn't make sense. Was this fantastic story investigated?'

'No.'

'I'll bet it wasn't,' averred Biggles. 'Your people in Polynesia have something better to do than chase wild geese, dogs, or whatever these creatures are supposed to be.'

'Why should we chase them?' enquired Marcel. 'We expect you to look after your property.'

'You'd have shouted loudly enough if one of your nationals had been chewed up by these alleged hounds, I'll warrant,' declared Biggles.

'Naturally,' replied Marcel, cheerfully. 'We expect people like you to see that their tenants keep dangerous pets chained up.'

'Are you coming with me to have a look at these beasts?'

'If I may. I'd like to see them. I have permission to go with you.'

Biggles nodded. 'This looks like being a real international turn-out. A Swedish colleague named Sven Heldersen is also coming with us.'

'*Bon.* Does he speak French?'

'I don't know. The important thing for me is, since I can't speak his language, he speaks mine. Now we'd better see about getting organised. We have a long way to go.'

That explains what the Sunderland was doing over the deep Pacific.

The call at Atuona had produced nothing tangible, but there were plenty of rumours. The dogs of Oratovoa were, Biggles was concerned to find, accepted without question. One man declared that a friend of his had been killed and eaten by them. Whether this was true or not one thing was certain. No Marquesan would go near Oratovoa.

The aircraft droned on, blue sky above and blue

water below, until a small dark hump crept up over the horizon straight ahead.

'As there's nothing else in that direction for thousands of miles, that must be the lump of rock we're making for,' said Biggles. 'Well, chaps, we should soon know all the answers.'

'What's the drill?' asked Ginger, for so far Biggles had said nothing about what he intended to do when they reached the island.

'I'll decide that when I've had a closer look at the place,' answered Biggles. 'I'm still keeping an open mind about the whole business. I shall probably take the obvious course of flying round the coastline at a low level to see if anyone's about. It shouldn't take us long to discover if there really are people living here. Ten minutes should be enough for that.'

'Unless the people go into hiding,' put in Algy.

'Can you think of any reason why they should hide themselves?'

'Frankly, no. But if there is any truth at all in these rumours I wouldn't expect to find people behaving normally.'

'If there are people hiding in the jungles you'd be wasting your time trying to winkle them out,' stated Marcel positively.

'I wouldn't try.'

'What if we can find nobody here, old boy?' queried Bertie.

'In that case there'd be no point in staying here. We'd toddle off back the way we came – unless anyone feels like taking a stroll at the risk of making dog's-meat of himself.'

The Sunderland droned on, the outline of Mystery Island hardening with every passing minute.

Chapter 2

MYSTERY ISLAND SHOWS ITS FACE

All eyes were on the Island as the flying-boat, now with its engines throttled back, lost altitude as it glided towards the isolated cone of earth that projected from a boundless expanse of sapphire sea. In general appearance, as Marcel remarked, it might have been one of the Marquesas they had so recently left.

With a final landfall of only two or three hundred feet of height Biggles opened up again, and running in close on even keel began to cruise along the coastline.

'Watch for smoke, or perhaps a flag, particularly near the water's edge,' he said. 'If there's anyone here that's where he should be.'

Mystery Island, now revealing its features at close range, to Ginger looked anything but inviting. On the contrary, its aspect was forbidding, repellent. With the exception of the inevitable coconut palms it had nothing in common with the low-lying atolls of, for instance, the Paumotus, which he had seen and on some of which they had landed. In a word, Oratovoa did not in the least conform to the popular idea of a South Sea island. From what he had heard of the place he had not expected that it would, but he was not prepared for anything quite as sinister as this.

Almost everywhere the great conical-shaped mass rose sheer from the thundering surf where blowholes spouted and hissed from a thousand wave-pounded caves and cracks. The summit, towering four thousand feet above, looked utterly inaccessible, for more reasons than one.

The lower slopes, where vegetation could secure a foothold, were buried under what appeared to be impenetrable tropical forest and jungle made up of the usual varieties of trees and shrubs tangled with interlacing vines of many sorts that had no beginning and no end. Through this riot of every shade of green burst the coconut palms, to wave their magnificent fronds in triumph. At frequent intervals sheer cliff broke through the herbage to provide perches for thousands of sea birds. These, disturbed by the unusual visitor, left the crags in clouds to keep it company, much to Biggles' annoyance, for he was often at pains to avoid collision.

Above the green belt, which followed the coast wherever it was possible, and varied in width from a few hundred yards to half a mile, the scenery was savage, yet, in a way, majestic. Much of it was sheer, perpendicular cliff, grey, purple and black, split, seamed and riven by frightful gorges and ravines. There were places where a cliff had collapsed to form huge landslides of debris, from pieces of rock the size of houses to long screes of smaller stuff. Sometimes these had torn a passage far down into the forest, piling the uprooted trees into a hideous mass of smashed and tortured timber.

There were places where even the colours of the cliffs looked unnatural, revealing streaks of strange metallic hues, the result, Ginger could only conclude, of having been subjected to fierce heat. Sometimes a long, silvery thread showed where water was making its way to the sea. Where waterfalls cascaded over the higher cliffs they swayed in the breeze like lengths of flimsy gauze.

The general impression thus created was one of unreality. To Ginger it looked a nightmare of a place. There was no beauty anywhere. Everywhere it was the same; a picture of nature in the raw, undisturbed, untamed. There was no smoke, or any other sign of human occupation. If there were animals, they saw none. Only the seagulls, large and small, that had made the desolate island their home, provided movement.

In a few minutes the aircraft had circumnavigated the island without seeing any change in the spectacle. There was only one beach worthy of the name, and that was a narrow crescent of dark grey sand behind the bay noted in Admiralty Sailing Directions. Even that was a depressing-looking place, lifeless and with nothing that Ginger could see to recommend it.

'I don't know what to make of this and that's a fact,' Biggles told the others in a puzzled voice. 'I can't believe there's anyone on this repulsive-looking dump. At least, I can't imagine any sane person living here from choice. Apart from anything else there's no contact with the outside world. Now that planes fly over the Poles it must be the loneliest place on earth.'

'What about castaways?' suggested Algy.

'If so why haven't we seen them? They must have heard us even if they couldn't see us. Why don't they show a flag or make smoke? No. Had castaways been here surely they would have made their home on that beach, where they could bathe, catch fish for food, and be handy to make contact with any ship that called.

They certainly wouldn't be sitting on top of the beastly place. They'd find nothing to eat there. I'd say those rumours we've heard are a lot of humbug.'

'So what do we do next, old boy?' enquired Bertie.

'One thing we can't do is footle about burning petrol looking for we don't know what,' answered Biggles.

'Aren't you going to land?' queried Ginger.

'I don't feel like putting down in that bay,' returned Biggles. 'We were warned against rocks and I could see water breaking on some. This is no place to rip our keel open and be stuck here until the Air Commodore sends someone along to find out what became of us.'

'What about that inlet which is supposed to run far into the island?' said Sven. 'I didn't see it.'

No one had seen it.

'There must be something of the sort here unless it's been choked by rocks falling from above,' said Biggles. 'We'd better have another look. I'll cruise round again, a little higher. Keep your eyes open.' He began another circuit.

This time, perhaps because the machine was a hundred feet higher, or because they were watching for a definite object, they found the fiord. That it had not been observed on the first circuit was no matter for surprise, for it ran in at an acute angle behind a mighty buttress of rock.

Biggles took the machine through the opening and there before them was a long stretch of calm water coloured green and black by the reflections of the rising ground on either side. A few rocks projected from the placid surface but they were widely spaced and therefore easily avoided. Biggles said he would go down for a rest, something to eat and a cigarette.

A moment later the Sunderland's keel was cutting a broad V on the water. The aircraft ran quietly to a stop at what they imagined to be the end of the inlet, to find that this was not the case. It was only a bend. Beyond it the narrow waterway continued for some distance at a width that diminished gradually from one or two hundred yards to a mere point.

Biggles taxied on with short bursts of throttle, holding to the middle of the fairway and keeping an anxious eye on the steepening cliffs that occurred at intervals on either side; for, as he remarked, some of the rocks looked so precariously poised that the vibration of the engines might be sufficient to bring them down. Even if they didn't fall on the aircraft they might set up a swell sufficient to carry them into trouble in a place where there was little room to manoeuvre.

'This seems to be it,' he said at last, taking his hand from the throttle and allowing the flying-boat to run to a standstill resting on its reflection on the dark water. He switched off. The airscrews stopped. An uncanny silence fell, for here, out of the wind, even the trees were still. The only things that moved were some gulls that had followed them in. The only sound their melancholy cries.

'Well chaps, it looks as if we've come a long way for nothing,' said Bertie, cheerfully.

'Apart from the bay this is the only place where I'd expect to find anyone,' observed Biggles, taking out his cigarette case.

Ginger climbed on the hull and cupping his hands round his mouth let out a hail. 'Ho there! anyone about?'

The result, as the echoes came back and retreated, startled him, as did some ripples large enough to denote the presence of a big fish in the water. He surveyed the sides of the gorge, more from casual curiosity than in expectation of seeing anything that could be associated with their quest. But an object caught his eye and held it. He moved to a new position and looked again, long and carefully. Then, abruptly, he returned to the cabin. 'Hold your hats, everyone,' he said, tersely.

Biggles looked up. 'What is it?'

'I believe I can see a vessel of some sort a little higher up.'

Biggles sprang to his feet, his expression changing. 'You believe! Aren't you sure?'

'Not absolutely. All I can say is, I can see a bit of what looks like the stern of a small yacht. If it is a ship it's pretty dirty. I can't see the whole of the thing because a low, jungle-covered headland sticks out and comes between us. I fancy there's a sort of awning, or what's left of one, over the afterworks. It was a piece of the stuff flapping that first caught my eye.'

'We'll have a look at this,' asserted Biggles. 'I shall be surprised if you're right. A ship means a crew, and had there been anyone on board he must have heard us.'

'He would certainly have heard me hail,' said Ginger.

'Maybe he doesn't want to be seen,' put in Marcel. 'Maybe that's why he tucks himself behind the headland – *hein*?'

They went out on to the hull and Ginger pointed to the object that had claimed his attention.

It took Biggles only a moment, after he had raised his binoculars, to make up his mind. 'You're right,' he said, crisply. 'It's a ship. There's a chance, of course, that it's only an old abandoned hulk. We'd better have a closer look.'

He went to the controls and restarted the engines. Then, feeling his way at slow speed he moved the machine forward.

In two or three minutes all doubts were settled. Riding at an anchor behind the headland, only a short distance from a shelving beach of detritus, was a small yacht, dirty and weather-stained but, as far as could be judged, seaworthy. There was no one on deck, and some gulls sitting on the roof of the wheelhouse suggested there was nobody on board, either.

With the others standing on the hull, or in the open doorway, watching intently, Biggles took the aircraft right up. 'Anyone aboard?' shouted Ginger; but there was no reply. Not that one was really expected. The vessel was not a hulk, but it had an abandoned look about it.

Ginger regarded it suspiciously, for there is always something sinister, some hint of tragedy, about an abandoned ship.

Biggles joined the others as they stood trying to make out the name on the stern.

'*Dryad*. Rotterdam.' Algy read it out, letter by letter.

'That's the craft belonging to those Dutch film people,' reminded Ginger.

'So this is where she ended up,' remarked Biggles. 'There was truth behind that rumour, anyway.'

'If one tale is true the others could be true,' opined

Marcel.

'Those two naval vessels that came to have a look round must have missed the inlet,' said Biggles. 'That's understandable. Maybe the skippers wouldn't risk running close inshore for fear of the rocks. That'd be understandable, too.'

'Where could the people have gone?' queried Sven. 'Certainly there is no one on board.'

'No one alive, anyhow,' returned Biggles, meaningly. 'We shan't solve the mystery standing here. Get aboard, some of you, and see what you can find. The log-book may tell us what went wrong. That something must have gone wrong is quite obvious.'

Ginger walked along a wing, and reaching out grabbed the rail and pulled himself aboard. The others joined him, except Biggles, who remained at the controls of the aircraft.

'This ship was at sea not so very long ago,' observed Sven, confidently, as they looked about them.

'Well, there's no one on it now, and by the look of things I'd say it was some time ago that this deck was last swabbed.' Ginger eyed the two lifeboats, canvas shrouded, still on their davits. 'How did the people get ashore?' he queried.

'They may have been towing a dinghy,' offered Algy.

Ginger's eyes explored the tiny stony beach, less than fifty yards away. 'Whatever they used to get ashore that's where it should be,' he said. 'I don't see it.'

'Never mind that. Let's go below,' returned Algy.

They separated, each to explore as he felt inclined.

Ginger made for the companion-way and went down, not without qualms, for he was fully prepared to find signs of tragedy. But all appeared to be in order – with one exception. He failed to find the log-book. He hunted for it in every likely place but in the end was forced to the conclusion that it wasn't there. He returned to the deck to find the others. Biggles, having made fast, was coming aboard.

'Where's the log?' was Biggles' first question.

'I can't find it,' reported Ginger.

'But it must be here!'

'It isn't. I've looked everywhere. Search for yourself.'

'Hm. That's queer.' Biggles looked around. 'Anyone else anything to report?'

'The engine seems to be all right and there's plenty of oil in the tanks,' said Marcel.

'What is it? A diesel?'

'Yes.'

'They couldn't have been short of water,' volunteered Sven. 'There's a modern distillation plant below. That would make them independent of calls merely for water.'

'How about grub?'

Bertie answered. 'Not much. A few tins of biscuits. Enough, perhaps, to have seen them back to the Marquesas.'

Biggles frowned. 'They could hardly have been as low as that when they came here.'

'I fancy you're right, old boy. There's a lot of paper and packing stuff kicking about as if there had been a spot of looting. And I can tell you this. There isn't a bottle of booze of any sort on board, which on a craft of this sort strikes me as a bit odd – if you see what I mean.'

'Anyone raiding the stores would be pretty certain to

lift any grog that might be about.'

'Absolutely, old boy, absolutely.'

All standing together on deck they discussed the mystery.

'If the people aren't on board they must have gone ashore; and if they went ashore they must still be there, alive or dead,' Biggles said. 'It could be either. But why they should all go ashore leaving no one in charge of the ship beats me. People don't do that sort of thing.'

'Why take the log with them, anyway?' said Algy. 'People don't normally do that, either.'

'Well, as they're not here they must have gone ashore, however strange that may seem,' declared Biggles. 'They didn't leave by water because the boats are still here and there's nothing on the beach. As far as exploring is concerned that's the only way they could have gone.' He pointed to a gloomy-looking track running back steeply from the stony beach. With branches interlaced overhead it looked like a tunnel. Vines sprawled about over what was obviously boggy ground.

For a little while they stood there, subjecting the landscape, what little they could see of it, to a close scrutiny.

'I don't get it,' muttered Biggles at last. 'But I'm beginning to wonder if we haven't treated this whole business a bit too casually. There's something queer going on here, or has been going on, but I haven't a clue as to what it could be. People don't abandon their ship in a dump like this for no reason at all. Has anyone any idea?'

No one had an idea. However, Marcel pointed out

that they had only seen the island from a little above ground level and suggested it might be a good thing to make a survey from above. 'These people may have decided to climb to the top of the rock and then found they couldn't get down.'

'Why not?' asked Biggles. 'If they could get up they could get down.'

'They might have started a terrible landslide and been cut off.'

'That's possible, although it doesn't seem very likely,' conceded Biggles. 'But that still doesn't explain why they should take the log with them.'

'We might as well give the beastly place the once over now we are here,' said Bertie.

Biggles agreed. 'That's about all we can do. Ships have of course been abandoned in mysterious circumstances before today, but this certainly is a puzzler. The *Dryad* said it was coming here. As we see, it got here. Then what happened? Where do we go from there?'

'There's only one answer to that and it sticks out a mile,' declared Algy. 'The crew went ashore and ran into trouble.'

'But the log! Why take the log?'

'It's my guess they didn't take it. Someone came later and collected it. Possibly the man who helped himself to the stores.'

'Maybe that's the answer. He may have taken the log so that should a search party arrive and find the yacht they wouldn't have a clue as to what had happened. But that poses the question: if the man who took the log didn't want anyone to know what had happened why did he leave the yacht here? Why not scuttle her and make a thorough job of it? He'd only have to open the sea cocks.'

'Maybe he had an idea of using the yacht later on,' suggested Sven.

'We're going round in circles,' asserted Algy. 'We're doing a lot of guessing and getting nowhere. Why not give the place a complete combing from up topsides and have done with it?'

'Fair enough,' agreed Biggles. 'It's the only thing left to do. Let's get on with it.'

The flying-boat was taken slowly back down the narrow channel to the open sea, but only after Biggles had made a close examination of the water in front of him did he take off. He did not climb directly to the summit of the central peak, but keeping near the slopes, wound his way upwards in a spiral so that close watch could be kept for signs of human occupation.

If the picture presented from a lower level had been one of rugged grandeur, the same sight seen from close range was breath-taking. Everywhere frowned insurmountable precipices, some overhanging and looking as if a touch would be enough to send them crashing into the forest below. Needles of rock that had split from the main body stood erect like the spires of a cathedral. Of what the rock was actually composed could not of course be determined. At the foot of the numerous landslides lay great piles of dead wood, apparently trees that had been torn from their roots by the downrush of hundreds of tons of rock.Once above the belt of tropic vegetation the island was a place of desolation. Below the aircraft now were two definite rings; the first, of surf, being white, and the second, where the trees and shrubs had obtained a foothold, mostly a vivid green.

'I'm not much for mountain climbing at any time but I'd hate to drag myself to the top of that ugly-looking pile,' remarked Biggles once, as they neared the summit and saw a mass of rock break off for no reason at all that they could see, and go thundering down into a yawning ravine.

'I would bet no one has ever been to the top,' said Marcel. 'Only a madman would attempt it. The heat would be formidable.'

'Too bally hot altogether,' said Bertie.

'How could it be otherwise, being practically on the Equator,' reminded Biggles, as he drew the control column back a little to take the aircraft to the top of the peak.

For a minute nobody spoke. Everyone stared, brows furrowed with amazement. No guess had been made as to what might be expected at the top, probably because it was generally assumed that the peak would be like most mountain tops – a point or a ridge of bare rock. At all events, that was what Ginger had visualised. Wherefore to say he was dumbfounded as he now gazed down would hardly describe his sensations. And that, judging from their expressions, applied to the others.

The centre of Mystery Island was a crater, obviously made when the original volcano had blown its heart out. It was not very deep. Roughly oval in shape, as was the island itself, it might have been a little over a mile long and half that width at the widest place. That in itself was not particularly remarkable. Indeed, from what they knew such a formation might have been expected. The shock came from finding the crater inhabited. That was immediately apparent, for not only were there buildings – a row of houses and several detached structures – but people could be seen moving about, some near the buildings, others working on ground which, from the colour of the crops and regularity of the boundaries, was clearly under cultivation. The ground was anything but level. There was a general slope towards the centre so that some terracing had been necessary. There were rocks everywhere.

Biggles was first to speak. 'Well – well – well,' he murmured. 'I thought I was too old to be surprised by anything, but this, I must admit, shakes me to the roots. What the deuce is going on here?'

'Perhaps we've discovered an unknown tribe,' offered Ginger, hopefully.

'Unknown fiddlesticks,' returned Biggles. 'Those houses are modern, and most of the people down there are white.'

By this time the aircraft was gliding, losing height, so that everything was in plain view.

'*Sacré bleu!*' exclaimed Marcel. 'As you English say, what do you know?'

Biggles answered. 'One thing I know is, it will be some time before we satisfy our curiosity. There's no place up here to land. I didn't imagine there would be. Not that I thought we'd have any reason to land. If we're to get a closer view of this fantastic set-up it will mean doing what I said a minute ago I wouldn't do. We shall have to walk up.'

'But I say, old lad, you're not seriously thinking of doing that?' said Bertie, looking aghast.

'At the moment I'm hardly able to think at all,' admitted Biggles. 'My head is still in a spin. But we shall have to think about it sometime. For a start we'd better get back to the inlet and give our brains a chance to function. One thought that does occur to me is this. Had no one come here in an aircraft those people on the roof might have been there till doomsday without anyone knowing anything about it.'

By the time he had finished speaking Biggles had throttled back and was gliding down to the inlet. The only remarks made on the way were repeated expressions of astonishment and disbelief.

Biggles landed, ran on a little way into the fiord and came to anchor near the abandoned yacht.

'Now,' he said, turning in his seat and lighting a cigarette. 'Will someone please tell me what's going on up there?'

He waited, but it seemed that no one was prepared to offer an explanation.

'No ideas?' he questioned, looking round.

'Not a clue,' said Algy, and the others shook their heads.

'All right,' said Biggles. 'Rustle some grub, Ginger. There's no reason why we shouldn't eat.'

Chapter 3

THE JUNGLE PATH

They finished their lunch of 'hard tack', biscuits, bully beef and jam. Ginger made a pot of coffee and there they sat, door and ports open, for the heat, even in the shade, was stifling.

'This business now boils down to what these people are doing here,' remarked Biggles.

'I would have thought it mattered more *who* they were,' said Sven.

'You mean their nationality?'

'Yes.'

Biggles shook his head. 'Oh no. I don't care two hoots about that. I judge a man by what he is, not by the country in which he happens to be born. Provided he's straight he can be any nationality under the sun, and profess any religion he likes, as far as I'm concerned. There's nothing to prevent anyone from living on this, or any other South Sea Island, as long as he doesn't get into mischief.'

'It's hard to see what sort of mischief the people here could get into,' put in Algy.

'Some people would get into mischief anywhere,' asserted Biggles.

'The island is too far away from any air or shipping route to be of use as a military base, with the possible exception of aviation.'

'Aviation is out of it,' declared Biggles. 'A helicopter would have to take chances to get down in that crater, never mind a jet.'

'How about a secret radio station?' suggested Ginger.

'I looked for wireless masts but I couldn't see any,' said Marcel.

Sven joined in the argument. 'These people are up to no good.'

Biggles turned to him. 'What makes you think that?'

'If they had nothing to be afraid of, or ashamed of, surely they would have come down to call on us. They must have seen the plane, and even if they hadn't watched it the sound would have told them it had come down.'

'You may have something there,' agreed Biggles.

'If they don't come down, how about dropping a message to them asking what they're doing?' offered Ginger.

'That's no use.'

'Why not?'

'Because if they're up to some funny business they're not likely to tell us about it.'

Ginger shrugged. 'Okay. So what are you going to do about it?'

'What it really boils down to is this,' answered Biggles. 'We can either go home and report what we've seen or we can sweat up to the top of that hill to find out for ourselves what goes on. And when I say sweat I mean drip. It's hot enough sitting here doing nothing. I'd wager you could fry bacon and eggs on that rock, exposed to the sun.'

'If we go home merely to report there's a colony on

the island, some smart guy will want to know why we didn't find out, while we were here, who the people are and what they're doing,' stated Algy, morosely.

'Absolutely. How right you are, laddie,' murmured Bertie.

Biggles also agreed. 'We would probably be sent back to finish the job. It would be a waste of time trying to describe the conditions here to people who have never seen the place. It would be no use saying we couldn't get to the top. The answer to that would be, if other people could get up there what was there to stop us going up.'

'What is there to stop us going up, if it comes to that?' asked Sven.

Biggles replied. 'Nothing, I suppose, except that I'm a pilot, not an Alpine guide. To hoof it to the top of that lump of rock would be no ordinary hike. It would be tough enough for people who knew their way. We don't know the way, and from what we've seen it would be no easy job to find it. These rocks are rotten. You can see that from the number of landslides. I don't want to finish up by rolling down one of those thousand foot screes into the sea.'

'Don't forget the dogs, old boy. Don't forget the jolly old bow-wows,' put in Bertie.

'Oh, I'm not worried about that,' rejoined Biggles, casually. 'I'm only thinking about dragging my bones to the top of that hill in a temperature of around a hundred and ten, sweaty heat, at that.'

'It must be like a stoke hole in that crater,' Algy said. 'Still, they must like it or they'd come down. If they wanted to get away there's a perfectly good yacht waiting to take them.'

'I'll tell you what,' said Biggles, with an air of having made up his mind and tossing his cigarette end into the water. 'We must at least make an attempt to get to the bottom of this – or, as it seems, to the top of it. We couldn't get to the crater today if we tried; there isn't time; and I'd hate to be benighted half way. We might make an early start tomorrow before the sun gets too blistering. Meanwhile, instead of sitting here sweltering in our own juice we might as well see if we can find any sort of path. There must be a track somewhere.'

'That looked like the beginning of one behind that bit of a beach beyond the yacht,' said Algy. 'Maybe that's why the yacht's there.'

'It'd be the most likely place to find a path,' replied Biggles. 'There aren't many places where one could get ashore and if there is a track it's bound to start from one of them. Let's go and have a look. It won't do us any harm to stretch our legs, anyway.'

'We could collect a few bananas, any old how,' declared Bertie, cheerfully. 'I saw some beauties.'

'Plantains,' corrected Marcel. 'Wild bananas, really. They grow everywhere in the Marquesas. They're much bigger than the ordinary banana.'

'How lovely,' said Bertie. 'I'm all for big bananas.'

'Don't try swimming ashore,' advised Ginger.

'Why not?'

'There are some pretty hefty fish in the drink. I saw them.'

'Sharks?'

'I don't know what they were.'

'There are always big fish round Pacific islands,'

stated Marcel. 'Size doesn't mean they're dangerous.'

'There's no need for anyone to risk making shark-fodder of himself,' said Biggles. 'I'll move up to the beach and take the boat in to wading depth. Who's coming ashore? There's no need for us all to go. Someone will have to stay with the aircraft, anyhow.'

Marcel looked at Biggles. 'Are you expecting trouble?'

'No, but in these waters a squall can blow up at short notice. Besides, the people up top might send someone down with a message, or to find out if we've landed.'

'I'll stay aboard,' volunteered Algy. 'I'm nothing for jungle-trotting. I've had some. That forest may look like fairyland from here but I'd bet it's as full of biting bugs as an egg is full of meat. Let them go as likes it. I'll stay here. When Bertie has finished stuffing himself with bananas he can bring me a bunch.'

They made ready to move.

Biggles started the engines and nosed the machine on past the yacht before turning in to the so-called beach, which was really no more than a short, narrow strip of stones, caused, probably, by the tide scour round the headland. He went on until the keel scraped gently on the bottom. Then, switching off, he led the way ashore through water no more than knee deep. Stooping, he picked up a handful of the brash of which the beach was composed.

'Pumice-stone,' he said. 'Pretty rotten stuff at that. Rock, with all the life taken out of it by fire. There must have been a time when the whole place was red hot.'

'Chase me round the gasworks! The bally place is hot enough now,' remarked Bertie, mopping his brow with a handkerchief already damp.

Biggles turned his back to the water and crunched his way over the stones to the tunnel-like gap in the forest. The ground was covered with trailing vines, but there was no doubt about it being a track. At all events, there was no other way of advancing, for the thicket on either side was an almost solid tangle of ferns, trees, and flowering shrubs, the perfume of which mingled with a stench of rotting leaves into which feet sank at every step.

'This track must have been cut at the time the island was occupied by Polynesians,' said Marcel. 'It would need an army of men to do it. You can see where even big trees were felled to make a way.'

A thin buzzing became audible and an instant later Ginger slapped at an insect that had settled on his bare arm. 'My gosh! Can that little beast bite,' he complained, bitterly. 'Algy knew what he was doing when he offered to stay on board.'

'It was a *nono*,' informed Marcel. 'I was afraid we should find some here. They're not dangerous but they're a pest on all the Marquesas. You can't do anything about them.'

'Just let them help themselves to a lump of meat when they feel like it,' muttered Bertie, striking furiously at his neck, on which an insect had settled.

'Exactly,' answered Marcel, grinning. 'You soon get used to them.'

'The little devils bite like dogs,' swore Ginger, snatching up a small branch and lashing the air.

'Talking of dogs, I don't see any,' remarked Biggles. 'The boys who reported 'em must have got 'em mixed up with *nonos*,' retorted Ginger.

Biggles stopped, looking hard at a heap of dead vines that had been piled beside the track. 'What's all this,' he murmured. He picked up a stick and poked it into the pile. It struck something hard. Throwing aside the stick he seized the vines with both hands and tore them aside. The keel of a dinghy was exposed, the little boat being upside down.

'So now we know how the crew of the *Dryad* came ashore,' he said evenly. 'Far from helping us, that only makes their behaviour more difficult to understand. Why pull the boat up here, and why hide it? – for that obviously was the intention in smothering it with all this stuff. The answer is, of course, the Dutch people didn't do it. Not by the widest stretch of imagination was there any reason why they should do such a thing. No. Somebody else had a hand in this.'

'There are no oars here,' informed Sven, who had tilted up the boat.

'Which means somebody decided to put the boat out of action.' Biggles pursed his lips. 'Okay. Let's go on a bit.'

They did not go far. Biggles stopped again, looking at something that lay in the path. It was a big bunch of plantains. The fruit was beginning to rot. He examined the end of the stalk. He looked at the surrounding trees. There was not a plantain among them.

'Somebody cut these,' he announced. 'And he didn't cut them here. Which means that the man who cut them was carrying them. Why did he cut them and then throw them away?'

Nobody answered.

Biggles went on. 'We needn't go much further,' he decided. 'We've learned what we wanted to know. This is a track. It has been used fairly recently. It must lead to somewhere, and we can only suppose it goes right on to the top.'

He took a few more paces, peering ahead in the dim green light that filtered through from above. He stopped again, looking hard at some whitish objects that lay scattered among the dead leaves underfoot. A few slow paces took him to them.

'This isn't so funny,' he announced, grimly. '*Nonos* didn't do *that*.'

There was no need to say what *that* was.

Lying about were bones. That they were human bones was proved by a skull. Also lying on the ground was a ragged length of material decorated with a broad flower design. Nearby lay another rotting bunch of plantains.

'This man was a Polynesian, probably from the Marquesas,' said Marcel, in a tone of authority. He touched the cloth with thc toe of his shoe. 'That was a home-made garment many of them wear called a *pareu*. The stuff is *tupa*. It's made from the inner fibres of the breadfruit tree. This wretched fellow met his death here. He was killed, eaten, and from the way the bones are scattered about, literally torn to pieces. He dropped the plantains, which no doubt he came here to gather, when he was overtaken.'

'He wouldn't be likely to come here alone,' said Biggles.

'Oh no. There were probably several men in a canoe.'

'Another one of the party hung on to his plantains for

as long as he could, but had to drop them lower down.'

'Exactly. If this is what can happen here no wonder Oratovoa has a bad name on the Marquesas so that the men seldom come here now.'

'This,' said Biggles, seriously, 'puts a different complexion on the whole business. I'm thinking of the crew of that yacht. If a Marquesan, who should be at home in the forest, can lose his life like this, the same thing could happen to a European.'

'Without a doubt.'

'What could have done it?'

'This was the work of a wild beast,' said Marcel. 'There are no wild beasts on the islands. There are pigs that have gone wild. They will eat anything. They wouldn't kill a man; but if they found a dead body they might pull it to pieces. Also there are a few cats, but cats wouldn't do this.'

'There was no reason why this man should die here.'

'No reason at all. I'd say he was killed by the creatures that devoured him.'

'What about the dogs?' said Ginger. 'We were told there were dogs here.'

Biggles nodded. 'I was waiting for someone to say that. It begins to look as if there might be something in that story after all.'

Hardly had the words left his lips than from somewhere in the jungle came a low, ferocious growl.

Chapter 4

REPULSED

'That was a dog,' said Ginger, as they all stood staring in the direction from which the sound had come.

'It certainly wasn't a *nono*, old boy. At least, I should jolly well hope not,' stated Bertie, brightly, making it clear that even now he saw nothing serious in the situation.

'I suppose there could be a stray dog here,' remarked Biggles, casually.

Marcel shrugged. 'It is possible. *Pourquoi pas?*'

'What's an odd dog, or even two,' said Ginger, carelessly. 'Let's get out of this. I've had about enough of these *nonos*.'

'The trouble is, the little blighters haven't had enough of us,' went on Bertie, slapping the back of his hand.

From this light-hearted conversation it was evident that none of them anticipated serious trouble from an animal like a dog, which is always assumed to be more or less domesticated. An unarmed Marquesan might be vulnerable to attack, but not a party of armed Europeans.

They were still standing, peering this way and that for sight of the animal, prompted perhaps more by curiosity than any other reason. Biggles took out his automatic. 'I'll give him a fright if he shows himself,' he announced.

As he said later, it didn't occur to him for a moment that he might have to use the gun. He thought the report, when he fired, would be enough to frighten the creature. Aside from that he felt helpless. One can't fight a dog, even a small one, with bare hands, without risk of being hurt; and this was no place to suffer a bite which, if it drew blood, could have dangerous after-effects. In the tropics wounds do not heal easily, and even a scratch, if ignored, can quickly become septic.

There is no doubt whatever that had it not been for the warning growl a very serious situation would have arisen. As things were, Biggles was ready for the attack when it came; but he was certainly not prepared for the ferocity with which it was launched. Nor, in fact, could any of them have imagined what was about to happen. Ginger was thinking of one dog only, but he took the precaution of providing himself with a stick from a fallen branch.

Happening to glance up the track a movement in the half-light caught his eye. He stiffened. 'Look out!' he exclaimed tersely. 'There he is! What a brute!'

On the path had appeared a dog of the Alsatian type. It was in a crouching position with its lips rolled back to show its teeth. Actually, to Ginger it looked more like a big Canadian timber wolf than a dog. It had that cold, relentless look of hate in its eyes. In fact, he would have been sure it was a wolf had he not known that wolves do not occur on South Sea islands.

'Watch your legs, chaps, that doggie means business,' advised Bertie. Even now from the way he spoke it was obvious that he did not suspect the sort of business in which he was soon to be engaged.

Neither, for that matter, did Biggles. Looking at the dog he pointed an accusing finger at it. 'Get off home, you,' he ordered, in the sharp tone of voice that most dogs understand.

The animal did not obey. Its answer was to creep slowly nearer, legs bent, stomach to the ground. Then it came on with a rush, which ended with it taking a flying leap at Biggles' throat.

Perhaps still thinking of the brute as a dog Biggles hesitated to use his gun. Or it may be that, taken by surprise, he hadn't time. Taking a quick, instinctive pace backward, he met the charge in mid-air with his arm, fetching the dog a swinging swipe that sent it rolling into the scrub beside the track. But it was on its feet again in an instant, snarling horribly as it came back at him.

'Shoot! You'll have to shoot,' almost screamed Ginger.

Biggles did not need the advice. By this time he had realised that half-hearted measures would not suffice to deal with an attack that was not mere intimidation. Jumping sideways to dodge the gnashing teeth he fired a point blank into the animal's side just behind the shoulder. It was enough. The dog rolled over and lay twitching in its death agonies, with Biggles, his face pale, staring at it as if he couldn't believe his eyes.

For a few seconds, stunned to silence by shock, nobody spoke. Then, looking up, Biggles said: 'I hope there aren't many of those brutes about. By thunder! He nearly caught me on one foot.'

'Well, you gave him what he asked for, old boy,' said Bertie. 'There's only one thing to do with a rogue who behaves like that. My trouble is,' he added plaintively, 'in this heat my bally eyeglass gets all steamed up.'

Biggles did not answer. He was still staring at the animal, obviously shaken by the suddenness and savagery of the assault, when Marcel called, shrilly: '*Attention*! There are more coming.'

The warning brought everyone to the alert.

'We'd better get back to the boat,' decided Biggles, shortly.

But before they could move three dogs had appeared on the path. Two were Alsatians. The other was a rough-coated, broad-chested type, rather like a chow. Rustlings in the jungle on either side made it clear that more were on the way. Somewhere in the undergrowth a dog bayed like a hound.

'Come on. Let's get back,' ordered Biggles again, crisply. 'I don't like this. There are too many of them.'

They began to back down the path, pistols ready for use; but it was soon apparent that the order to retire was easier to give than obey. Dogs began to break cover not only higher up the track but behind them. Suddenly there were dogs everywhere, some silent, some snarling or growling. Bertie's gun crashed, and one that had made a run at him limped away, howling. Marcel shot another, while Ginger, who was still carrying his stick in his right hand, fetched yet another a crack across the muzzle with a force that produced a yelp of pain. He dropped the stick and prepared to use his automatic. He hated doing it, but he perceived that this was no time to be squeamish. The situation was fast becoming desperate. If the dogs were determined to behave like wild beasts, he thought, they would have to take the consequences.

The party was now retreating down the path with as much speed as it could make, which was not as fast as they could have wished. It was not easy. For the most part they had to walk backwards on the slippery track in order to keep their faces turned to the main attack, which was coming down the hill above them. In spite of casualties the dogs became more instead of fewer. Fortunately some stopped to tear at others that had been killed or wounded, in the manner of wolves. There was no longer any question of firing over the animals' heads in the hope of frightening them. It was a case of making every shot tell.

With a thrill of horror Ginger realised how the wretched Marquesan had been killed. A man, or men, practically naked, and without firearms, would have no chance at all. He also realised that they were lucky in that they had not far to go. Had they been attacked higher up the path they never would have got back, for by the time the beach was reached they were practically out of ammunition. The result was a final rush into the sea. Even then they had to wade waist deep, for some of the dogs followed them into the water. One swam towards Biggles. But there it was out of its element, and Biggles put his last bullet between its hate-filled eyes as it opened its mouth to bite him.

And there they all stood, with Algy shouting from the aircraft asking what he should do, while thirty or forty dogs of different breeds and sizes tore up and down the beach snarling and mouthing with fury. It struck

Ginger that the animals really were mad. There were pups among them, making it evident that the beasts were breeding, so the pack would get larger instead of smaller.

Not until they had waded along to the aircraft and climbed on board did anyone comment on this desperate adventure. Algy, of course, had heard the gun shots and seen the reason for them.

'Has anyone been bitten?' Biggles asked anxiously.

It turned out that clothes had been torn, but by great good fortune, helped by the fact that they had carried firearms, no one had actually been bitten. Sven had had a narrow escape with a long scratch down his leg. Blood had not been drawn but Biggles dressed it with strong iodine from the medicine chest.

'Well, that was a nasty business,' said Biggles, philosophically. 'I suppose we should have paid more attention to the tales we were told. I wonder what ails those dogs.'

'I've met some stinkers in my time but nothing like that lot,' declared Bertie. 'I never thought the day would come when I'd have to start mopping up a pack with a gun.'

'We couldn't do anything else,' said Biggles, simply. 'A dog that behaves like a wolf must be treated like a wolf. I took that tale, told by the Marquesans, about being set on by dogs, with a pinch of salt, but all I can say now is they were lucky to get away. Had we not had our guns on us we should have been in a pretty mess.' He turned to Marcel. 'Is this the normal behaviour of dogs that have gone wild on the islands?'

'It has been known to happen that they have turned

savage but I've never heard of anything on this scale,' answered Marcel, looking puzzled. 'Some time ago there were rumours of wild dogs hunting on the top of Hiva-oa, one of the Marquesas. People used to go up to tap the wild rubber that grows on the plateau, but the dogs made it too dangerous. It was impossible to sleep at night. It was necessary to light a big fire and sit by it. That was the story. I didn't pay much attention to it, having no reason to. I've never heard of wild animals, dogs, cats or cattle, coming down to sea level.'

'I only hope this doesn't account for the disappearance of the Dutch people who came on the yacht,' said Biggles, looking worried. 'If they went wandering up that path with nothing more effective than a camera in their hands – well, anything could have happened to them.'

'Maybe it's the dogs that prevent the people up top from coming down to the sea,' surmised Ginger.

'That's what I've been wondering,' said Biggles. 'But there's another angle to that. Those dogs might have been turned loose with the definite object of discouraging visitors.'

'What makes you think that?'

'I feel there are too many dogs for the pack to be accidental. We killed several, but there must have been close on forty on the beach at the finish.'

'That raises the question, which were here first, the people or the dogs,' put in Algy. 'I don't see how the people on top could have got there had the dogs been here in force when they arrived.'

'And now they're there they can't get down on account of the brutes,' contributed Ginger.

Biggles shook his head. 'I don't think that's the answer. Don't you remember that in the tale we were told about the dogs there was mention that a man heard shouting. It was a minor point at the time, but it now suggests to me the possibility of the dogs being under control. That is to say, they can be let out and allowed to run wild but will go back to kennels when told to do so. This machine must have been seen when we flew over the crater. If it was realised that we had landed, what more natural – if my theory is correct – than that the dogs should be freed to prevent us from getting far ashore. Years ago they used to keep packs of hounds to hunt down runaway slaves.'

'Are you suggesting that the same sort of thing could be happening here?' asked Sven.

'I don't know. Something of the sort, perhaps.'

'But look here, old boy, tell me this,' requested Bertie. 'First of all, why should the johnnies on top have any objection to anyone landing? Do they think the bally place belongs to them?'

'That,' said Biggles, 'is what I intend to find out.'

'But how are you going to get past the dogs?'

'The dogs will have to be shot.'

'But you can't shoot dogs in cold blood,' protested Ginger.

'These are not ordinary dogs,' retorted Biggles. 'I'd put them in the same category as dangerous wild beasts. From the way they behave they might as well be tigers. Make no mistake, they're man-eaters. We've seen some of their work. They will have to be destroyed by somebody, some time. They can't be allowed to go on like this. Anyone is likely to land here. We know of one canoe-load of Marquesans who were driven here by a storm. They were lucky enough to get back to their canoe otherwise we wouldn't have heard about it. I'm afraid another lot weren't so lucky – or not all of them. We saw the bones of one on the path. That could happen again. The island is British so the responsibility is ours, and before I leave here I shall see to it that this sort of thing doesn't happen again. If nothing is done the brutes will completely overrun the place. Whether they got here by accident or whether they were put here makes no difference. Are they still on the beach?'

Ginger looked out of the window. 'Yes. Some of them.'

'It is my opinion that these dogs were put here deliberately,' said Marcel.

'I'm inclined to think so, too,' returned Biggles. 'Look at the breeds. Alsatians and chows. Both heavy types. Both can be savage. How could they have got here by accident? People have been known to take a dog cruising with them, but not that sort. No large ships come anywhere near. A trader might call, but what trader would clutter himself up with a hound that needs a pound or more of meat a day to keep it fit? Actually, as this island has been uninhabited for years a trader has no reason to call. The only people likely to come are locals; looking for water, plantains, coconuts, bread-fruit or perhaps wild vanilla beans. Once in a while a shipwrecked sailor might come ashore. Once in a blue moon a yacht like the *Dryad* might put in. Wherefore I say that as to our certain knowledge these dogs are killers they'll have to be destroyed, as they would be at home. It will be a nasty business but I can see no alternative.'

The others reluctantly agreed.

Biggles stood up. 'Look at 'em,' he muttered, and all eyes went to the beach where the animals were either squatting on their haunches, tongues lolling, staring at the aircraft, or pacing up and down like caged lions.

'Pass me the rifle,' Biggles told Ginger. 'Let's get on with the beastly business.'

While the others stood watching the beach while they waited for Ginger to bring the rifle from its locker, suddenly, quite clearly through the sultry air, came a shrill whistle; or rather, a series of short sharp blasts. The sound came from the jungle well up the flank of the mountain, but it was not possible to locate it exactly.

That the dogs had heard the whistle, and understood what it meant, was evident from their behaviour. Those that had been sitting sprang to their feet, and presently, with many a backward glance, the whole pack was on its way back up the path. In a minute there was not a dog in sight.

'Never mind the rifle,' Biggles told Ginger. 'We shan't need it – at any rate for the moment, although I have a feeling we shall want it before we're through with this crazy business.' He looked at the others with a curious expression on his face. 'So now we know,' he said simply.

'What do we know?' asked Algy.

'These dogs are under control. They didn't get here by accident. They were brought here. They've been trained to hunt – and kill.'

'Men,' said Ginger, quietly.

'What else is there to hunt?'

'And what are you going to do about it?'

'Find the huntsman, of course.' Biggles smiled faintly. 'I don't know how we're going to do it, but this murderous racket can't be allowed to go on. For that's what it is – murder. By thunder! No wonder the Marquesans are giving the place a wide berth. Well, we'd better do some hard thinking.'

Chapter 5

BIGGLES DECIDES

'We've got tangled up in some queer jobs in our time but this one certainly is a corker,' remarked Bertie. 'Blow me down! I'm all for a spot of huntin', but not this sort. Dog huntin' on a South Sea island. By jove! That's a new one. What sort of a lunatic asylum is this?'

'It doesn't look like a lunatic asylum to me,' rejoined Biggles. 'It looks more like a carefully organised death trap. I wouldn't try to guess what's going on here but someone is determined to prevent anyone from landing.'

'Or from getting away,' said Marcel, shrewdly.

'As you say, or from getting away,' agreed Biggles. 'It could be either or both. Whichever it is it has got to be stopped. The answer as to how that's to be done won't come to us sitting here. We shall have to find the people responsible, and that, I fancy, will mean climbing to the top of that perishing mountain. I'd as soon be kicked as try it.'

'How are you going to do it, anyway,' enquired Algy. 'You'll never get through that wolf-pack on the path.'

'I've no intention of attempting it. I'm not asking to be mauled. We shall have to find another way up. That's all there is to it.'

'There may not be another way.'

'Surely there must be. This beach where we landed is

probably the usual point of disembarkation. The Marquesans knew of it. We know they came here. One at least lost his life on that path. People have no doubt used that landing for generations. That, of course, is why the dogs are there. But I can't believe there are enough dogs to guard every line of approach to the top. That would require hundreds of dogs. Dogs don't live on bananas or coconuts. A cat can keep itself, but not a dog. These dogs have to be fed. We shall have to find a way where there are no dogs.'

'That looks like being a stiff proposition,' said Algy. 'You can't walk round the coast because it's either sheer jungle or cliffs. And to taxi round, in a heavy swell with rocks sticking out of it like dragon's teeth, would be asking for it.'

'Even if we could walk, to leave the machine here would be inviting our friends up top to come along and scuttle her,' put in Ginger.

'Don't think I can't see the difficulties,' said Biggles. 'Instead of everyone telling me what we can't do, how about someone telling me what we can do.'

'There are two lifeboats on the yacht; how about using one of them for cruising round the coast,' suggested Sven. 'We shall have to explore.'

'That's better,' said Biggles. 'I can't say I'm infatuated with the idea because it would need seamanship to keep a small boat right side up in that surf and that's not in my line. Still, we might try it. Even if a squall did blow up, the machine should be safe in the inlet.'

'I'm not so sure of that,' said Ginger, who was still regarding the beach through a window.

'What do you mean?'

'I have an uncomfortable feeling that we're being watched. Two or three times I've seen bushes move as if someone was prowling in the jungle. Once I thought I caught a glimpse of a face, too.'

They all watched for some time but saw nothing to confirm Ginger's suspicions.

'I don't like this at all,' said Biggles, looking worried. 'If these people ashore are capable of setting a pack of hounds on visitors, and the way it's being done is plain murder, they're capable of any devilment. They have only to damage the aircraft and we've had it. They must know we're here so it would be natural for them to come close to have a look at us. I'm afraid this knocks the boat idea on the head. They'd see us take it and guess what we were doing.'

'Unless we took it after dark,' put in Marcel.

'They'd hear us. We couldn't get a boat on the water without making a sound. Wait a minute, though. We might be able to get over that. I was going to move the aircraft, anyway. We're too close to that beach for my liking. If these people really mean trouble they could rush us. We'll take the machine to the widest part of the fiord and find a mooring on the far side. To save starting the engines, and using petrol which we may need before we get home, we'll take one of the *Dryad*'s boats and tow her over. That would serve a dual purpose. If we were seen taking the boat it would be supposed it was for that purpose.'

'How are you going to get to the yacht without starting the engines?' asked Ginger.

'Swim.'

'Not for me,' declared Ginger, emphatically. 'I'm not making shark-meat of myself for anybody.'

'The poor brutes have to eat,' protested Marcel.

'Fair enough,' agreed Ginger. 'I'm just taking good care that they don't eat me.'

'Sharks are rarely as dangerous as some people imagine.'

'Don't give me that,' sneered Ginger. 'Anyone would think you liked sharks.'

'I have the greatest admiration for them,' confessed Marcel. 'If there's one creature in the world that was fashioned perfectly for the life it has to lead, it's a shark. Sheer bone and muscle. And when it comes to streamlining it has the best aircraft designers beaten to – how do you call it? – a frazzle.'

'Okay. You can have —'

'Oh, for goodness sake,' broke in Algy, impatiently. 'What's all this rot about sharks? If we're going to do anything let's get on with it and stop nattering about sharks as if they were film stars. We've only about half an hour of daylight left, and you know how it is. Once the sun dips night comes down like a blanket. At the rate we're going, by the time we decide to move we shall be carrying half a ton of barnacles.'

'I'll swim over to the yacht and fetch a boat,' said Marcel, getting up. 'It's no distance.'

The gap between the flying boat and the yacht was in fact about fifty yards.

Marcel threw off his clothes except his underpants and diving in struck out for the yacht at a fast stroke. The others watched breathlessly, and with relief saw him reach the objective and pull himself aboard. He went to the first lifeboat, looked in it, and went on to the second. One glance and he was on the rail. A dive, and he was on his way back. Nothing happened. The others pulled him in through the open door.

'No use,' he said, wringing the water from his hair.

'Why not?'

'There are no oars. They're gone.'

'I should have guessed that,' muttered Biggles. 'They're determined no one shall get away. After seeing the dinghy we might have foreseen that the boats would be out of action. That settles it. I'm not staying here. We're too vulnerable. We'll find a safer mooring.' He closed the door and went through to the control cabin.

'Where are you going?' asked Algy.

'Back down the inlet a little way.'

'If we go on fiddling about like this we shall find ourselves without enough petrol to get anywhere,' stated Algy.

The engines came to life, and the big flying boat moved majestically down the creek, edging towards the far side. It went on to the widest part, and there, with enough way on the ship to keep it just moving, Biggles cut the engines again.

'Get a line to the shore, one of you,' he called. 'Make fast to a tree – anything. Buck up.'

The need for urgency was evident, for darkness was closing in, as Algy had said, like a curtain falling from the sky. And there were rocks about. Bertie and Ginger splashed their way ashore, taking a line, making for the only open spot, which was the base of a narrow scree. Actually, it formed a tiny rocky beach.

A few minutes' work and they were once more

assembled in the cabin.

'Of all the daft operations this is the daftest,' muttered Algy.

'It may look daft to you, but it wasn't so funny to some of the people, who tried to get ashore and ran into those dogs,' retorted Biggles, with asperity. 'Unless I'm barking up the wrong tree murder has been done here, and a very nasty kind of murder, too. I don't like that, and before I leave here I'm going to find out who's doing it, and why. Make some coffee, Ginger.'

Ginger obeyed with alacrity, for he saw the mood Biggles was in.

'You know, old boy, I believe we could get ashore here,' remarked Bertie.

'Up through the jungle?'

'It didn't look too bad to me, from what I could see of it in the twilight.'

'It'd be an awful long way from here to the top even if that was possible,' said Sven. 'It would mean going round the far inside end of the inlet. We're on the wrong side of it here.'

'I don't care how far it is,' replied Biggles. 'We're not pushed for time. I don't know how I'm going to do it but I'm going to the top of that mountain – somehow.'

'Bravo!' murmured Marcel, his dark eyes smiling. 'I am coming with you. *Bon.* It will be an affair to remember.'

'That's what I like to hear,' said Biggles, approvingly. 'In the morning we'll have a look at things. With any luck we might arrive at the crater at a spot where these dog merchants won't be expecting us. Tonight we'll mount guard. There are six of us so that will only mean two hour spells. We'll draw for the order presently.'

Ginger put the coffee on the case used as a table.

They continued talking for some time and then drew lots for guard duty. Bertie drew number one and went outside to watch. The conversation of the others became desultory and one after the other they settled down to rest.

Ginger was awakened at midnight for he had drawn the middle watch. Without a word to Marcel, whom he relieved, so as not to waken the others, he went out on to the hull and found a seat. It was, he found, a weird experience, sitting there alone, in the dark, the only sounds the distant roar of the surf and a lesser noise he took to be the splash of a waterfall on the side of the mountain. At first he could see practically nothing. Occasionally a fish jumped, or a shoal being pursued by one, starting ripples of green phosphorescent fire on the surface of the inlet. This was nature left alone, as it had always been. The place induced such sombre thoughts. The stars seemed to hang low in the sky.

Just before the end of his tour of duty a crescent moon swept up above the cliff to flood the fiord with a pale, silvery light, which did nothing to enliven the scene. Inky spires stood stark and grim against the sky while one by one coal-black ravines came into view. The effect was to make the place look evil. It might have been dead, but Ginger knew it was not. A cloud came along, spilling rain, but the atmosphere remained humid. Ginger took off his clothes and had a shower-bath. Everything dripped. But all the time he watched the far side of the fiord, particularly in the direction of the yacht. He saw nothing, and at two o'clock by his watch he went in to call Algy to take over.

Dawn, sunny and rainwashed, but with wisps of mist clinging to the cliffs, found them all on the move. No one had anything to report. Nothing suspicious had been seen or heard. Ginger made coffee and put out biscuits, sardines and tinned marmalade.

Biggles had gone outside, taking the binoculars, to study the slope for a possible route up, for he had no delusions about what the going would be like through the forest and jungle.

'I think it might be done,' he said at last. 'It would of course be an exhausting job. The dog route is no doubt the only easy way; that's why it's there and why the dogs are there; for the rest, there's not much in the way of choice. I imagine it would be all about the same.'

'And having got up there what are you going to do?' asked Algy. 'I have a feeling you wouldn't be popular.'

'That wouldn't be a new experience,' returned Biggles, dryly.

'Then you've definitely decided to go?'

'I shall have a shot at it. The alternative is to go home, and I don't feel like doing that, with the job half done.'

'Who will you take with you?'

'I shall ask for volunteers. Two will have to stay with the machine. As second in command you'd better be one of them, to take charge of the aircraft should the shore party not come back. But don't do anything in a hurry. I fully expect it will take us at least a day to get up there and another to get down.'

'That means humping food up with you.'

'And water,' said Biggles. 'I wouldn't rely on the stuff

we might find on the way. But let's get some breakfast and pack our kit.'

They went in. Biggles announced his decision. Everyone wanted to be in the party so Bertie had to be detailed to remain behind with Algy. With the possibility of finding French and Swedish nationals in the crater it would be necessary to take Marcel and Sven to act as interpreters, Biggles explained. Everyone would have to carry food and water, and be armed in case there should be trouble. Apart from that it would only be necessary to carry first aid medical equipment, and knives to cut a passage through the jungle should that be necessary.

Breakfast over, all hands were soon busy at their tasks, and in half an hour the party was ready to move off.

Chapter 6

THE LONG CLIMB

The sun was dispersing the wisps of grey mist that still clung to the sides of the mountain when the shore party, shouldering their loads, set off on what they knew would be an arduous task, one likely to test their endurance to the limit even if proved successful, which was far from certain. It consisted of Biggles, Ginger, Marcel and Sven.

Biggles' final orders to Algy and Bertie were simple, and subject to their own discretion. All being well they were to remain where they were, keeping a close watch for possible interference. Should circumstances arise to make the position dangerous they would of course have to move to another mooring. Should there be the slightest risk of losing the aircraft, their lifeline with civilisation, they were to take off and make for Australia from where they would be able to report by radio to the Air Commodore and ask for instructions. In the event of the shore party failing to return in four days they were to do that anyway. That, said Biggles, was the outside limit of the time they would be away if all was well with them. Should those on the mountain see the aircraft in the air they would know that the present mooring had been abandoned. Biggles thought that from the upper, open slopes, of the mountain, he would be able to keep an eye on the aircraft, or at least hear the engines should it move.

In point of fact the first part of the journey up the slope was not as bad as had been expected, this being due to the presence of big, heavily-leaved trees, which discouraged the growth of almost everything under them with the exception of moss and ferns. The worst obstacle was the state of the ground, which was a mixture of greasy mud and rotting leaves into which the feet sank to the ankles, making progress slow and laborious. However, as Biggles said cheerfully, they couldn't have it all ways.

Everything dripped moisture. There was nothing like a track so they were obviously breaking new ground. If there were any birds in this forest they did not see them. The only animals were guinea-pigs, of which there were plenty. And, of course, there were *nonos*, with their infuriating pin-pricks. Against these there was no protection. They were a trial that had to be suffered.

In an hour, maintaining a diagonally upward route, the party had climbed to an estimated height of five or six hundred feet and had moved perhaps half way to the inside end of the creek. Here the big trees gave way to sheer jungle which called often for the use of knives, and in which it was not easy to keep a straight course. Fortunately this belt was not very wide. It thinned towards the top and eventually gave way to fairly open ground. Presently, reaching a little plateau, they found themselves on the brink of a deep declivity, a sunless gulf in which the tree tops fell away steeply into depths still half hidden in steamy mist. Here Biggles called a halt for the first rest. Mud-plastered and streaming with perspiration they were all in need of one.

'We should demand double pay for this sort of graft,' muttered Ginger, irritably, as he flopped down.

It was a gloomy, lonely place in which they now found themselves. The only sound was the trickle of water as it splashed over an unseen cascade somewhere below. Being on the same side of the inlet as the aircraft they couldn't see it, but in the middle distance, through gaps in the trees, were patches of blue sea. Ginger discovered that the seat he had selected, which he had taken to be a rock, was the crumbling remains of an idol, evidently a relic of the people who had dwelt on the island in days gone by. They had more sense than to stay here, he thought moodily.

Biggles gave them ten minutes and then resumed the climb, still heading diagonally uphill, which again meant that tiresome way of walking with one leg higher than the other. Being closer to the summit, and under it, they could no longer see the actual peak, only the nearer ledges, grim and forbidding, inhabited by colonies of sea birds.

They were soon clear of the jungle, with the going becoming progressively steeper. There were no more *nonos*, which, as Biggles remarked, was something to be thankful for. The earth and leaf mould underfoot had now turned to rock; not hard, firm stuff, but rotten lava that crumbled when trodden on, producing a feeling of insecurity. Nothing felt really solid. Nor, in fact was it. Pieces often broke off, sometimes to roll down the hill. These, as they rolled, knocked off more pieces, so that the air was full of the sound of little landslides. Nowhere was the treacherous stuff to be trusted. Once a piece weighing half a ton broke off under Biggles' weight to go crashing down into the forest far below. Only by a cat-like leap did he save himself from going down with it. He made no comment, but turned a wry face at the others. The perilous conditions were plain for all to see.

Things became worse as the ascent continued, what from below had looked like solid rock revealing itself to be as porous as coke. It was the colour of coke, too, and it struck Ginger that there had been an eruption at no very distant date. A faint smell of sulphur was sometimes noticeable.

Biggles stopped, pointing at a thin miasma of misty smoke that drifted sluggishly from a ravine not far below them. 'Listen, chaps, and I'll tell you something,' he said, seriously. 'The fellow who reported this volcano as dead couldn't have looked very close. The people living in the crater need their heads examining. One day, and I'd say it could happen at any time, this place is going to do a Krakatoa,* and that'll be the end of it.'

To make matters more difficult the way was now barred with increasing frequency by the precipices and screes that had been observed from the aircraft when it had flown round the island. To get round these detours were necessary, with the result that progress became slower. They had to skirt ravines. And all the time there was the uncomfortable feeling that the ground on which

* Krakatoa was the island in Indonesia, between Java and Sumatra, which, in 1883, blew up with a roar that could be heard thousands of miles away. Where there had been a peak a thousand feet high became a chasm. An estimated 35,000 people lost their lives. Other volcanoes thought to be extinct have done the same thing.

Author.

they were standing might collapse and drop them into an abyss.

Perhaps even more alarming were the frowning crags overhead, and more than once Ginger stopped to regard them askance before tip-toeing under them, holding his breath until he was past the danger spot. The sun was now well up and the heat, striking down with full equatorial force, became a torture. All that Biggles had said about sweat had been justified, thought Ginger, who could feel perspiration trickling down his body in little rivulets. The air being humid, the body moisture did not evaporate as he had known it do in the dry heat of desert regions. However, as Biggles observed, at least there were no dogs to worry about. But there were other dangers.

It was while they were crossing a small, harmless looking plateau of grey pumice-stone, without any sort of vegetation on it, that Marcel broke through what was evidently a thin crust and sank up to his armpits. The others, lying at full length to distribute their weight, helped him out. Having rolled clear he rose up to regard, with a stream of vituperation in his native language, a mass of sulphur-reeking mud that clung to the lower part of his body. It was one of those occasions, no serious harm having been done, when spectators find humour in the misfortune of a companion. They smiled. Ginger laughed.

But Marcel saw nothing funny in the incident and he said so in no uncertain terms. He also gave his opinion of the expedition in general.

'Are you grumbling?' enquired Biggles.

Marcel said he found plenty to grumble about.

Biggles spoke seriously. 'Oh, come, Marcel. If you go on like that you'll develop into one of those miserable types that want everything easy, expecting everything to open and shut for them. Eventually they get that nothing is ever right. This is an experience, and experience is the sauce that gives life a flavour. Who wants to spend his days trotting along in the same old groove, seeing the same people and doing the same thing like a donkey on a beach? If you're going to leave the beaten track the first thing is to make sure you've got your sense of humour with you.'

'But I stink like a skunk,' protested Marcel.

'It'll wear off,' promised Biggles. 'I own that this particular jaunt seems a bit grim at the moment, but think how we shall laugh about it one of these days when someone says: do you remember the time we sweated up that pile of filthy rock called Oratovoa and Marcel fell into a pothole of muck. We shall laugh and laugh and laugh. Dash it! I could laugh now, and so would you if you could see yourself.'

They all started to laugh, and presently the crags echoed with their laughter, sending the gulls wheeling.

'That's enough,' said Biggles at last. 'We'd better push on.'

They resumed their toil, and after another hour of sheer hard labour the party reached another small plateau overlooking the inlet and perhaps two thousand feet above it. Being in line with the end the full length of the inlet was in view, with the aircraft, still at its mooring, looking like a tiny model floating on a sea of blue ink. Biggles called another halt, and with a gasp of thankfulness Ginger dropped his load and sank down beside it. There was a little grass, harsh, spikey-looking stuff, but at this altitude they were at least above the range of the *nonos*.

There were some pools of stagnant, nasty-looking water, and investigation revealed these to be as unpleasant to the taste as they were to the eye. Apart from a strong chemical flavour the water smelt strongly of bad fish, the result, Ginger supposed, of seagulls nesting on the ridges above. There were eggs, whole or broken, everywhere. In such intense heat water was vital, and they had to resort to their water-bottles. Somewhere above them, although it could still not be seen on account of intervening crags and ridges, was the summit. Biggles said he reckoned they were about halfway to the top.

After a rest of a quarter of an hour or so the march was continued. The spectacle presented of the towering cliffs around them was now magnificent, but it is unlikely that any of them were in a state to appreciate it. All the time the going was becoming steeper with conditions underfoot deteriorating. Progress was made by zigzagging. Feet either crunched into the volcanic ash or slid as the stuff gave way like loose gravel. It was like going the wrong way on an escalator.

Ginger was worrying about the return journey, for more than once he heard an avalanche behind them, as if the ledge they had just crossed had broken away bodily, thus cutting off their retreat. Sometimes he looked at Biggles questioningly, hoping he would reconsider what they were doing; but nothing was said about turning back. In his heart, of course, Ginger knew Biggles would not turn back. While progress was humanly possible he would carry on, however hard the labour or perilous the conditions. Biggles was like that. He hated this sort of thing as much as any of them, but having started he would not give up.

At every turn now Ginger was fully prepared to find their way barred by something impassable. It nearly happened several times, but somehow they always managed to scrape through. The end appeared to have come when a ravine yawned at their feet. There was no way in sight of getting round it. All around was a world of sheer and utter desolation of red and black honeycombed rock devoid of any sort of vegetation. Biggles took a coin from his pocket. 'Heads to the left, tails to the right,' he said, tossing it. 'Heads,' he announced, and set off to the left, following the brink of the chasm.

After half an hour of gruelling labour they came to the base of a landslide composed of giant rocks from which projected at all angles hundreds of long-dead trees that had been uprooted. To get over it was obviously out of the question. Biggles must have realised it, for he merely said, 'Nothing doing,' and turning about set off in the opposite direction. Ginger was appalled that all their labour had come to nothing but there was no alternative. In another half-hour they were back at the spot at which they had struck the ravine. Biggles didn't stop. He went right on. The others followed wearily.

After going some way the sides of the ravine began to draw together, and there was a hope that presently they would meet. They never did. The ravine ended abruptly in a sheer drop of a thousand feet. Without a word Biggles turned back to a place where the two walls had come so close together, a matter of only six or seven yards, that they were actually joined by a slender strip of rock, arched in the manner of a bridge. Biggles considered it reflectively. 'Pity we didn't bring a rope,' he said. 'No matter. We shall have to manage without one.'

'You're not thinking of crossing that thing!' exclaimed Ginger, aghast.

'There's no other way.'

'You must be raving mad.'

'The alternative is to admit we're beaten and go back to where we started from, having had this awful sweat for nothing.'

'Okay. So let's go back. I'd do anything rather than trust myself to that horror.'

Biggles smiled wanly, perspiration making little white lines down his grimy face. 'I'll admit it doesn't look inviting, but having come so far I'm going on,' he said. 'I'm not asking anyone else to come. You can all please yourselves about that. We knew we should have to take chances when we started. I'm the heaviest. If the thing will carry my weight it should hold for the rest of you. However, as I've said, you must please yourselves about that. If the bridge lets me down you'll have to go back anyway. Looking at it won't make it any stronger so let's see what the luck's like.'

So saying Biggles walked to the bridge.

Ginger closed his eyes. He couldn't bring himself to watch. Silence fell. A minute passed. He opened his eyes. Biggles was standing safely on the far side.

'Anyone coming?' he asked, casually.

Marcel said, '*Zut*! Never again will I go on a walking

tour with you.' He walked across.

Sven, somewhat pale, followed without a word.

Ginger braced himself. In spite of the heat his stomach seemed to have turned to ice. Staring straight in front of him like a sleep-walker he crossed the bridge and sank down on the far side.

'Nothing to it,' said Biggles, and walked on.

'We'll find some other way back if you don't mind,' said Ginger, as he rose to follow. 'One go of that is enough,' he added grimly.

'We can't have much further to go,' Biggles told him, cheerfully.

How far they went, following what looked like promising routes only to find their hopes dashed by some impassable obstacle, Ginger would not have attempted to guess. Sometimes it was a precipice, sometimes a wall of rock. Once a path ended in a point and they found themselves with nothing but empty space below. The sun was now directly overhead and Ginger was wondering for how much longer he could go on. Hanging over him, too, was the awful knowledge that having got to the top they would have to try to find their way down. Another worry was, the water-bottles were getting low. Frequent sips of water were necessary to replace the water lost by perspiration.

There was a horrible place where water running over rock had produced a green slime that was as slippery as ice. This was on a shelf only a few feet wide, where a fall would have meant plunging into a chasm. The murmur of the water that flowed over it could be heard in the black depths below.

They kept on, always making a little more altitude,

even though a detour sometimes meant going downhill a little way first. They came to a fantastic precipice which Ginger recalled seeing from the aircraft. It was, he reckoned, a drop of at least two thousand feet. Here they sat down for another rest, not to admire the view but because the ledge caught a little sea breeze. Far below, minute white specks which Ginger knew were gulls, drifted aimlessly. Where they were there seemed to be no life of any sort.

Near at hand began a giant's causeway of great blocks of black basalt. If this could be climbed, Biggles said, he thought it might be a short way to the top. The climb would be more or less vertical. He decided it would be worth trying.

A climb of three thousand feet or more is a stiff pull at any time. Here they were all near exhaustion. Ginger was prepared to take any risk to get the job finished. He tried not to think about the return journey. He was sure there was an easier path from the top to the sea, and vice versa. That, of course, was why the dogs were there. No man in his right mind would attempt what they had done, knowing what was before him.

The next half-hour was something Ginger knew he would never forget; but it achieved its purpose. The great rock landslide took them to the top. Not actually to the crater, but to the broad, comparatively open slope that formed the brim, a gentle incline on which grew a certain amount of grass and dwarf herbage. One of the plants, a creeper, carried small blue flowers. They could see the rim, a short distance away, hard cut against the sky. There was an open view on both sides. A fair breeze came off the sea.

'I think that's done it,' said Biggles, mopping his face and opening his shirt to allow the breeze to dry it. 'We'd better mark this spot where we came up in case we have to go back the same way. Meanwhile we'll have a breather. We've earned it.'

They rested for a little while and then set off on what appeared to be the last leg of their journey, following the edge of a deep ravine. The ground was not level as they had supposed. It was full of pits and potholes, although after what had gone before they were no more than a hindrance. Some of the holes contained water, presumably rainwater from the overnight shower. It was flat but drinkable, so they made the most of the opportunity to refresh themselves and top up their bottles.

'Hold hard,' called Ginger suddenly, stopping and staring along the open slope. 'There's a man. What's he doing?'

The others halted to watch. 'He looks like a European to me,' said Biggles. 'What's that he's carrying?'

Marcel answered. 'Plantains. He must have just come up from the forest.'

At that moment the man happened to look in their direction and it was clear from his actions that he had seen them. He dropped his load, and after a brief hesitation he hurried towards them, sometimes running, sometimes walking briskly.

So anxious was he to speak that he began before he reached them. 'What people are you?' he called, speaking English with an accent.

'We're a British expedition,' informed Biggles.

'Did you come in that plane we saw?'

'Yes.'

'How did you get up here?'

Biggles pointed. 'We walked. That's the way we came.'

'I didn't know it was possible.'

Biggles smiled faintly. 'Neither did we. We took a chance.'

'Did you see any dogs?'

'No.'

The man came up to them, and Ginger observed that he was younger than he had imagined, the mistake being due, probably, to a short, fair, curly beard. He wore only a shirt, trousers, and a pair of canvas shoes badly in need of repair. He was thin, but looked fairly fit. His blue eyes went from one to the other of them in a manner that suggested a sort of cautious excitement.

'What are you doing here?' asked Biggles, curiously.

'I've been to fetch the plantains.'

'I mean, what are you doing on the island?'

Before an answer could be given Sven stepped in. 'You're Swedish, aren't you?'

'Yes.'

'What's your name?'

'Pruntz. Axel Pruntz.'

'What about the others who left Sweden with you? Are they here?'

'All except Martin Larsson. He was my friend.'

'What happened to him?'

'He was determined to escape. I haven't seen him since.'

Biggles spoke. 'Escape? Does that mean you're

prisoners here?'

'Very much so. Thank God you've come. I hope you'll take us away.'

'If you want to come with us you shall.'

'It won't be easy.'

'How many people are there here altogether?'

'I haven't actually counted them but there must be between twenty and twenty-five.'

Biggles pursed his lips. 'Who's keeping you here?'

'King Hara.'

'Is that his name or a title?'

'A title. We have to address him as King. He's mad.'

'All right,' said Biggles. 'We came here to find out what was going on. I suggest you sit down quietly and tell us.'

'You're not going to find it easy to believe.'

'We shall believe what you tell us.'

'You'd better keep watch, because if you're caught you're likely to stay here with us.' Axel spoke seriously.

'Who's going to catch us?'

'The guards. They're armed.'

'How many of them are there?'

'Ten, now that some of the prisoners have gone over to Hara's side for better treatment. They don't mind being here.'

'Tell us about it,' invited Biggles.

They all sat down near the brink of the ravine to catch the light breeze that came from the sea and Axel began his story.

Chapter 7

AXEL TELLS HIS TALE

'As far as I'm concerned the business began when I answered an advertisement in a newspaper asking for volunteers to develop a colony on a South Sea island,' stated Axel, speaking in English, after a few words in his own language with Sven.

'We know about that,' put in Biggles. 'I believe four people in Sweden accepted and left Stockholm in a yacht.'

'That is correct. The name of the yacht was *Liberta*, which, incidentally, is our name for this island.'

'You paid £500 each for the privilege of joining the project.'

'Yes.'

'Tell me at once, is this merely a racket for taking money off people?'

Axel hung on his answer. 'I wouldn't say that. When I've told you the whole story you'll be able to judge for yourself.'

'Go ahead. Just one other thing. There's a yacht below named the *Dryad*. It came here with a party of Dutch photographers.'

'That's right.'

'Are they here?'

'Yes.'

'You've spoken to them?'

'Of course.'

'Did they pay £500 apiece?'

'No. They knew nothing about what was going on here. But King Hara grabs anyone who lands, either because he's afraid of being reported or because it fits in with his scheme for establishing a colony.'

'What's the nationality of this man Hara?'

'He talks like an American. So do his friends, the people who help him to run the place. There are one or two Americans among the prisoners, too, curiously enough, although we are a mixed lot. There's a Chinese, a Jap, a Malay, some Polynesians and one or two I'm not sure about.'

'I see. Carry on.'

'After we left Sweden we picked up several other people who were mad enough to believe in the scheme – an Englishman and his wife, two Frenchmen – one young and one old – a Spaniard and several others. There were twelve of us by the time we got here. We also picked up stores, so that by the time we arrived we were loaded to capacity. Our last port of call was Papeete, in Tahiti.'

'So by that time Hara had picked up six thousand pounds.'

'I suppose so.'

'When you called at Tahiti you still had no suspicion that the scheme wasn't genuine?' questioned Biggles.

'I still wouldn't swear that it's a complete fraud. Conditions on board the *Liberta* were not bad. We had no complaints, except that we were a bit crowded. Martin and I were enjoying the adventure, and I think some of the others were, too. I was doing what I always wanted to do, make a long sea voyage to see distant parts of the world.'

'Was Hara on the *Liberta*?'

'No. We only met him after we got here. In charge on board the yacht was the skipper, a man named Ronbach. He's here now. He struck me as a queer type. That goes for the crew – but then, one wouldn't expect to find normal people on such a venture. It wasn't the *Liberta*'s first trip for colonists and stores. We learnt that from people when we got here. It wasn't until after we had left Tahiti that the atmosphere began to change. By then, of course, with no more ports of call, we were helpless.'

'In what way did things change?'

'The skipper became a domineering bully. It wasn't only that he made us work. I didn't mind that. It was the way he gave orders. Refusal to obey meant no rations. We didn't like that but there was nothing we could do about it. The attitude of the crew changed, too. Hitherto we had been treated like paying passengers, which in fact we were. Now the crew let us see they were the bosses. By the time we got here most of us had had enough and were wishing we hadn't come. We suspected there was a trick in it. When we reached the island, and saw the sort of place it was, we were pretty sick. It wasn't the sort of place we'd imagined.'

'I can believe that,' put in Biggles, dryly.

'I thought we were going to be marooned and left to get home as best we could, having lost our money; but I was wrong. We landed, and were made to march up that dreadful hill, carrying loads of stores. The crew carried nothing. They seemed amused by our indignation.'

'What about the dogs. Did you see them?'

'Yes, we saw them, but they didn't touch us.'

'Then they must be under control.'

'Yes. Two men, an American and a Mexican, have charge of them. They feed them, and set them on anyone who lands. Not that that happens very often. The real purpose of the dogs is to prevent us from getting down to the sea. There are more dogs here now than when we came.'

'What happened when you got to the top?'

'We were marched into the crater. You can imagine how we were feeling. We still didn't know what was in store for us. All we knew was that our beautiful dream of lying on a tropic beach nibbling coconuts had become a nightmare. When we got to the huts – there were no houses here then – Hara and his guards were waiting for us. Hara himself was dressed up like a king in a pantomime. He made a speech of welcome and told us that if we behaved ourselves we should be very happy, and so on, but if we tried to leave the place we would be punished – if we weren't torn to pieces by the dogs. He needn't have bothered to tell us because we soon learnt from the people already there what sort of trap we'd stepped into. We were prisoners with no hope of getting away. That's all there was to it.'

'Does this man Hara still insist that he's starting a colony?'

'Oh yes. We have our own flag – blue with a white star. It's hoisted every morning, with a ceremony.'

'You don't think Hara's idea is simply a way of making easy money?'

'He must have collected quite a lot of money even though some has been spent on stores, but I have a feeling there's more to it than we know even now. He says the plan is to make the island self-supporting. We've nearly reached that stage now, although the diet is monotonous. Cereals, mostly, with canned meat and vegetables once a week. I believe he wants this place for some purpose of his own. When we've served his purpose anything is likely to happen.'

'How long has this been going on?'

'Seven or eight years at least.'

'Where's Hara's yacht, the *Liberta*, now? I didn't see it below.'

'He's lost it. It was wrecked on its last trip. It returned here as a hurricane was blowing up and in trying to get into the fiord hit a rock and went to the bottom. The crew and most of the passengers got ashore by swimming. Two Americans were drowned. On that occasion the *Liberta* had been to the United States. We heard from the Dutch people that their yacht *Dryad* was below. We believe Hara seized them to get possession of the *Dryad* to replace the *Liberta*.'

'Tell me more about this man, Hara,' requested Biggles.

'I don't really know what to make of him,' confessed Axel. 'If he isn't mad he's a crank, unless of course he had a reason for running away from civilisation. He talks and can behave like a gentleman, but he can be a brute. He's a man of education. I should have told you he's a doctor. He was called Doctor Hara before he took it into his head to promote himself to King. He may or may not be qualified, but he certainly knows a great deal about medicine. My own opinion is, he was a professional doctor in the United States until either he got into some serious trouble or went queer in the head. What sane man would banish himself to a place like this? Sometimes I feel he only intends to stay here until he's collected a fortune. On the other hand, there's no doubt he's interested in what he calls his experiment.'

'What's that?'

'This colony idea. It won't be just an ordinary colony. He tells us that by mixing all the different types of men and women there will one day emerge a race of supermen combining the best qualities of them all. The original Polynesians, he says, were the perfect natural product of the islands, but because they had no immunity against the white man's diseases they died out.'

'That's true, anyway,' interposed Biggles.

'Hara says he hopes to repopulate the island with a mixture of black, Asian and white, that will have an inherent resistance to all diseases. In course of time, when civilisation has blown itself to pieces with atom bombs, such men could become rulers of the world.'

'He's nuts,' muttered Ginger.

'It is a fact that if any colonist develops anything like a malignant disease he disappears.'

Biggles frowned. 'Do you mean he's murdered?'

'I don't know. All I can say is he disappears. We never see him again. The last one to go like that was a Chinese, a nice chap named Ling-On. He showed symptoms of leprosy. The result of this is, if anyone is ill he daren't say so for fear of being put down like a sick dog or an old horse.'

'What does this man Hara look like?'

'He's about fifty, tall and well built. Going bald in front. Wears horn-rimmed glasses. You can't mistake him because he wears a crown.'

'A *crown*!' Biggles looked incredulous.

'Yes. A gold, or gold-painted, circlet. He dresses in a white robe like a bath gown, so that if it wasn't for his glasses he'd look like an ancient Roman emperor.'

'The man must have a screw loose, to say the least,' remarked Biggles.

'You wouldn't think so to talk to him,' rejoined Axel. 'He can talk about anything. He's well up in the classics and is fond of quoting them. If he's mad he doesn't suspect it.'

'No madman ever does,' returned Biggles. 'He has probably convinced himself that this experiment of his is all for the good of mankind.'

'Oh yes. He believes that. He makes no secret of it.'

'What do you colonists do with yourselves all day?'

'We have to work. People have different tasks according to their ability. Some build houses. That means crushing the rock to powder and mixing it with water to make a sort of cement. It is moulded into the shape of a brick and allowed to dry. Timber is brought up from the forest. Some people work in the fields, raising yams, maize, millet, and so on. The Frenchmen have a vineyard to tend. We are about to make our own wine. The women do the cooking. People like me are simply general labourers. One of my jobs is to collect plantains, bread-fruit and coconuts from the forest. That's what I was doing when I saw you.'

'What about the dogs?'

'I don't go down as far as that. The people in charge of the dogs have a hut near the inlet. They cut the fruit and two Marquesan assistants carry it to a point just above the forest. I pick it up there. It's a fairly easy path.'

'You believe there's only one way down to the coast?'

'That's what we're told. To try to get down any other way is certain death.'

'We found a way up. Bar accident we could get down the same way,' Biggles pointed out.

'I realise that. You can imagine my astonishment when I saw you sitting here.'

'Have you tried to escape?'

'If I had it's unlikely that I'd be here now. We prisoners talk of nothing else, but few have the nerve to try it. The trouble is, in this ghastly heat one soon loses the will to do anything. The crater is like an oven and it soaks all the energy out of a man. The big deterrent to escape is the fact that even if one reached the coast one wouldn't be able to get away. No ships call here. There was a time when a native canoe would put in, but the natives have got to know the place is dangerous and even they don't come any more. As far as I know, the only vessel that has been here in two years is this Dutch yacht, *Dryad*. If any other ships have come near we didn't see them. But then, one can't see the sea from inside the crater. It's like being in a pudding basin. As you can see for yourself, this is no ordinary island with a beach all round. There are only one or two places where it's possible actually to reach the sea, and they're patrolled by dogs. The rest is sheer precipice. One or two people have tried to escape but we don't know what became of them. That's how my friend Martin disappeared.'

'These people might be hiding in the forest,' suggested Biggles.

'It's possible. But what a life! They would be worse off than in the crater. They would be driven mad by the *nonos*. And they wouldn't dare to return to the crater for fear of punishment.'

'What about these guards? What are they like?'

'Awful. That of course is why they are what they are. Hara has two particular friends who appear to be in the business with him. They're second in command. They share his house. They're both Americans and presumably came here with him. One is Ronbach, who, as I told you, was captain of the *Liberta*. The other is a dreadful creature who talks like the gangsters in American films. His name is Swenson. I believe he was a crook wanted by the police. His face has changed since he came here. We think Hara has done something to it to make him look different.'

'You mean, by plastic surgery?'

'Yes. These two are in charge of the other guards. All these guards, by the way, are armed, and carry canes or whips.'

'In other words, slave-drivers.'

'Exactly.'

'What is the language spoken?'

'Mostly English and some French. People speak their own language when they're alone together.' Axel got up. 'But I must be getting along,' he said anxiously. 'I've stayed too long already. Guards will come looking for me.'

'Are you going back to the crater?' asked Biggles.

'Of course.'

'Why?'

Axel looked surprised. 'What else can I do?'

'Join our party. We have a flying-boat in the creek.'

'I know. We saw it yesterday. It caused great excitement. What are you going to do?'

'Ultimately, I hope we shall return to the aircraft. You could come with us. You would be a useful witness should this business go to court. But before I leave I want to see for myself what goes on in the crater.'

'If you go in you'll never get out,' said Axel, seriously.

'We'll see about that. One thing is certain. This racket will have to be exposed. This is a British island and if any flag is going to be flown over it, it will be the Union Jack. I don't suppose the British Government would have any objection to Hara or his cronies, or anyone else, staying here if they want to. But there can be no compulsion about it; slavery ended long ago. People who want to leave will be taken off. If they like to sue Hara for the return of their money, obtained by false pretences, that's up to them. This advertising for recruits will have to stop, too. The newspapers themselves will see to that when they know the facts.'

Sven looked at Axel. 'You should be able to recover your expenses by writing articles for the papers,' he said, smiling. 'You know – "My Life on a South Sea Island", and all that sort of thing.'

'All I ask is to get home,' said Axel, earnestly. 'I want to forget this, not remind myself by writing articles which no one would believe.'

'Well, are you going to stay with us?' asked Biggles.

'It's up to you.'

'Yes. Thank you. If I may.'

'How about slipping back into the crater and fetching some of your friends?'

Axel looked startled. 'That would be too dangerous.'

'How?'

'If anyone was seen trying to leave he would be shot.'

Biggles scowled. 'Are you seriously telling me that these guards actually *shoot* at people?'

'Yes. You don't seem to realise how serious this is. Only the other day I saw a man shot as he tried to run away. We were working in the fields. I think he must suddenly have gone mad. He threw down his hoe and made a run for it. The guards shouted to him to stop, but he didn't. He was shot.'

'By whom?'

'One of the guards fired two shots and missed. Swenson snatched the rifle away from him and shot the man dead.'

'Who was this man?'

'He was from Tahiti. We called him Pepe.'

'You actually saw this?'

'Yes.'

'In that case Swenson will stand trial for murder,' declared Biggles, grimly. 'If there has been killing here that puts a different complexion on the whole business.'

'*Attention*,' said Marcel, sharply. 'Someone comes now.'

Chapter 8

THE FIRST CLASH

All eyes switched to the direction in which Marcel was looking.

A man was standing clearly silhouetted on the skyline above them. He carried a long object over his arm. It looked like a rifle.

'He's searching for me,' said Axel, calmly, although his face had turned pale. 'I should have gone earlier. This will mean trouble.'

'I may have something to say about that,' stated Biggles. 'You know, Axel, I'm afraid you've let these people get on top of you. Pull yourself together.'

'But you don't know—'

'I can imagine.'

'He's calling.'

'Let him call.'

'What had I better do?'

'Do nothing. Let him make the first move. It'll be interesting to see what he does when he gets over the shock of seeing us here.'

'He'll know I've been talking to you,' said Axel, looking worried.

'Of course he will,' affirmed Biggles. 'What about it? From what you've told us you've got reason to talk.'

'He's coming down,' observed Ginger.

'Can you see who it is?' Biggles asked Axel.

'Yes. It's Swenson.'

'The man who killed Pepe?'

'That's right.'

Swenson, the rifle in the crook of his arm, approached slowly, as if he might have been trying to weigh up the situation. This gave those waiting ample opportunity to look at him.

He was a burly man, swarthy, black-bearded, with a truculent expression. He wore an open-necked shirt, white linen trousers and old tennis boots. A weather-stained panama was clapped low on his head. Reaching them he stopped, regarding with calculating eyes each member of the party. For a moment or two nobody spoke. Then Biggles said: 'Pardon my curiosity but what do you find up here to shoot?'

Swenson ignored the question. Speaking with a harsh nasal twang he enquired: 'Who are you?'

'For that matter, who are you?' returned Biggles.

'That's my business,' snapped Swenson.

'As a representative of the British Government to whom this island belongs, your business here also happens to be my business,' came back Biggles, succinctly.

'How did you get here?'

'I thought you might be curious to know that,' said Biggles, smiling faintly. 'We just walked up the hill.'

'What have you come for?'

'To find out what's going on here.'

'How are you going to do that?'

'I've done it.'

'How?'

'This young man has just told me all about it.'

Swenson glared at Axel. 'Squealer, eh?'

'It seems to me that he has good reason to complain,' said Biggles, evenly. 'And, by the same token, you have something to explain.'

'We'll see about that,' growled Swenson. He jerked a thumb at Axel. 'Come on, you.'

'Stay where you are, Axel,' said Biggles, quietly.

'You'll do as I tell you if you know what's good for you,' Swenson rasped, looking at Axel.

'If he knows what's good for him he'll stay here,' said Biggles, getting up. 'Aside from that, from now on I'm giving the orders here. Sit still, Axel.'

Swenson stared at Biggles. 'So you're giving the orders,' he sneered.

'That's what I said. You'd better go back to Hara and tell him I'm on my way to see him. He appears to have been doing as he liked here, but that's finished.'

'You're going to tell us what we can do?'

'I'm going to tell you what you can't do. Incidentally, be a little more careful how you handle that rifle. Point it where you like – but not at me.'

'Afraid there might be an accident, eh?'

'It could happen. I'm just warning you to see that it doesn't. Now, unless you have any more to say, I suggest you go back to your boss and tell him I'm on my way.'

For a little while Swenson stood looking at Biggles as if he couldn't believe his ears. Biggles' calm assurance may have been something new in his experience. Then he drew a deep breath and began slowly to walk away. But he didn't go far. Perhaps six paces. Then, whirling round, he swung up the rifle and fired.

Biggles moved just as fast. He jumped sideways and the crack of his automatic came within a split second of the report of the rifle. Swenson stumbled. He dropped the rifle to clutch at his shoulder, staggering backwards. Biggles shouted a warning. All the others leapt to their feet in alarm, for the wounded man had swayed perilously near the brink of the ravine, which apparently he had forgotten was there. There was no time to do more than that. Swenson went backwards over the edge. There were three or four seconds of brittle silence and they heard the body crash into the trees far below. With one accord they all ran to the brink of the chasm and looked down. Nothing could be seen of the man who had fallen. The only sound was the trickle of running water under the trees.

Axel turned a white shocked face to Biggles. 'You've killed him!' he said.

'I won't accept that,' answered Biggles, whose face had lost some of its colour. 'He was responsible for what happened. Twice he pointed that rifle at me and I gave him fair warning not to do it again. After all,' he went on bitterly, 'what am I supposed to do when I know a man contemplates murder? Stand still and let him shoot me?'

'*Mon Dieu!*' muttered Marcel. 'I never saw a man move faster than you did.'

'I was ready. I knew what he was going to do.'

'How?'

'From the way he held the rifle when he turned to go. Moreover, I saw in his eyes what he intended. He had been weighing up his chances all the time he was talking to me. When dealing with a man of that type always watch his eyes. He nearly got me, even so, and would have done had he taken time for a better aim. I felt the wind of his bullet on my cheek.'

'Are you going down to look for him?' asked Sven.

'We've no way of getting down.'

'You think he's dead?'

'He couldn't have survived that fall.'

'He may not have realised you had a gun,' said Axel.

'In that case there was even less excuse for what he did. It means he tried to shoot an unarmed man. From what you tell us, Axel, he's done that before. This time it didn't come off, and, frankly, I'm not such a hypocrite as to pretend I'm sorry for a man who, for no justifiable reason, tried to murder me. That's all I have to say about it.'

'Well, we've one villain less to deal with,' remarked Marcel, practically. 'What do we do next?'

'Pick up that rifle, Ginger, it may come in handy,' ordered Biggles. 'Particularly if there are any more up here of Swenson's type,' he added.

'What's the next move?' asked Ginger, as he obeyed.

'We'll go on and tell Hara what has happened.'

Ginger blinked. 'You're not thinking of going into the crater!'

'I shall have to, sooner or later. There's no hurry about it. I wasn't prepared for anything quite like this. The situation calls for some hard thinking. I suppose the sensible thing to do would be go home and report; but if we did that it might be weeks before official action was taken. We should be some time getting home. Then there would be discussions. More time lost. I don't suppose there's a British Naval craft within a thousand miles. We can't leave these unfortunate dupes of Hara here for weeks, perhaps months. In that time anything could happen to them. Let me think.'

Biggles lit a cigarette.

He thought for some time. Then he said: 'If this man Hara is as trigger-happy as Swenson it would be silly to order him to do what we have no power to enforce. It would also be unwise to leave ourselves without a line of communication with the aircraft. I'm thinking about those dogs. It seems likely that we shall have to go back the way we came. What I suggest, therefore, is this. I'll go on alone, or, if he'll come with me, with Marcel. I choose Marcel because there are several French nationals here. I propose dealing with the situation like this.' Biggles drummed his fingers on a rock.

'Ginger, you'll stay here, or out of sight a little lower down, and keep watch for us to return. You may have to cover our retreat if we come back with more haste than dignity. That could easily happen. You can have Swenson's rifle. Axel will stay with you so that you can take turns at resting. It may be convenient to keep him here anyway, because he knows his way about the crater and in an emergency could act as guide. Sven will return to the aircraft, report what has happened here and stand at alert all the time. If Marcel and I don't come back Algy will have to go for help, although I'd rather not do that if it can be avoided.'

'What do you think you and Marcel can do against that gang if they get tough?' enquired Ginger, a suspicion of sarcasm in his voice.

'There wouldn't be much we could do,' admitted Biggles. 'If I can get to this man Hara and talk to him I may be able to make him see sense. I shall tell him the game is up. He can't buck the governments of Britain, France, Sweden and Holland. Unless he really is out of his mind he'll realise that. If he was fool enough to bump us off he'd have to pay. If he'll listen to reason, all I shall ask is that he'll allow those people who want to go to leave without any fuss. That will mean calling off these infernal dogs. He himself, and those who want to stay, can carry on pending a decision by the government as to whether or not they should be allowed to remain here. That, of course, would mean him giving an undertaking to stop this dog racket, thus making the island safe for visitors. No one is likely to interfere with him in the crater. I can't say fairer than that. I realise I'm taking a chance in calling on a man who may be a lunatic, but nothing can be done unless I get in touch with him.'

'You can't knock sense into a madman,' said Sven.

Biggles agreed. 'I'd like to settle this affair without any more bloodshed, if it's possible. The alternative to handling the thing quietly would probably mean sending along a troop of marine commandos to take the place by force. That would start something. With the whole world on the boil and ready to scream at every little incident Oratovoa would become a headline in every newspaper. There would be questions asked at the United Nations. Some of these people, in fact, the ringleaders, are Americans. The U.S. government will scream if they're touched.'

'What about Swenson?' asked Ginger. 'I imagine he was an American.'

'He won't talk, much less scream,' replied Biggles,

grimly. 'He'll be the subject of a secret report when I get home. You all saw what happened. As for Hara, I don't see how he can say anything without implicating himself in what appears to be a bare-faced scheme for getting money under false pretences. Remember, those dogs have been responsible for the death of at least one man.'

'He could say they didn't belong to him,' Ginger pointed out.

'Axel would bear witness against that. I have a feeling that the Americans here, those who are here from choice, won't want to get involved with their government, who may know more about them than is good for them.' Biggles looked around. 'Has anyone anything to say or are we agreed on the plan?'

Nobody had an alternative scheme, although it was evident that they held Biggles' proposal to be risky, to say the least of it, even though, as he argued, he was an official representative of the British Government.

'All right, Sven,' said Biggles. 'You move off. You might just get back to the plane in daylight. Mind how you go.'

Sven set off towards the spot from which they had emerged to their present position and was soon out of sight over the brow of the hill.

Ginger shouldered the rifle. 'Come on, Axel, let's get in position,' he said. Then, looking at Biggles, 'How long are we to stay if you don't come back?'

'Give me twenty-four hours, anyway,' decided Biggles. 'If I'm not back by the end of that time you'll know Hara is being awkward, in which case you'll have to use your initiative. Your best plan might be to make for the aircraft and rejoin the others. Don't show yourselves over the lip of the crater in daylight. Your trump card is that Hara doesn't know you're here.'

'Okay.' Ginger went off, accompanied by Axel.

Biggles looked at Marcel 'Are you coming with me? Don't feel that you have to.'

'But certainly I shall come with you, old cabbage,' declared Marcel.

'Good. Then let's get along and hear what King Hara has to say for himself.'

They set off up the last incline towards the rim of the crater.

Before they had reached it, however, two men had appeared further along against the skyline. When they saw the visitors they turned and ran towards them. Biggles and Marcel, taking no notice, continued to walk forward without changing their pace.

It could soon be seen that the two men running towards them were dark-skinned, and since they carried canes were obviously two of the guards. They slowed down as they drew near, presumably at a loss to know what to do when they observed that the people coming towards them were strangers.

Coming within speaking distance one said: 'We heard shootin'.'

'You did,' confirmed Biggles. 'A man was shot.' He pointed. 'He fell into that ravine.'

'Who – who was this man?'

'A man named Swenson.'

'Who shot him?'

'I did. If he was a friend of yours you'd better see about finding him.'

From the way the men stared at Biggles with glassy eyes and sagging jaws it was clear that they found the situation beyond them. For this Biggles' off-hand manner may have been partly responsible. They stared at the ravine then back at Biggles.

'Where you goin'?' one managed to get out.

'We're going to see Mr Hara,' answered Biggles. 'Do you know where he is to be found?'

'Sure.'

'In that case you can show us the way to him. Lead on.'

'Sure. Sure,' said the guard uncomfortably.

Biggles smiled faintly and walked on.

Chapter 9

'KING' HARA

Biggles and Marcel, with the guards walking near taking frequent furtive glances at them, reached the top of the final rise, and there, falling away in a gentle slope before them, was their objective, the crater and the settlement hidden away inside it.

Biggles stopped to make a thorough survey of the place. It was clear that a considerable amount of work had been done and more was in progress: men were still working, sometimes alone or in pairs, and occasionally in little groups watched by their taskmasters. How they were able to do manual labour in such stifling heat posed a question, although according to Axel there was no alternative. It was a case of work or starve. The village, if the few permanent buildings could be so described, was a quarter of a mile further on, plain to see in the noonday sun. Sometimes a man walked from one building to another, otherwise there was no sign of activity.

'What do you make of it, old fox?' asked Marcel.

Biggles raised a shoulder. 'Had Axel not told us it would have been hard to guess. I'll keep an open mind about the real purpose of this establishment until I've had a word with the man who's running it. I'm not expecting to get much satisfaction from him because I suspect he's round the bend, as we say; but we must give him the benefit of the doubt. No normal man would live from choice in what must be one of the hottest spots on earth to say nothing of being one of the most difficult to reach. The man must either be hiding from somebody or something or we're faced with dealing with a fanatic. We should soon know the answer.'

They walked on, one of the guards now hurrying ahead presumably to give warning of their approach. Biggles did not attempt to stop him. The supposition was confirmed when the guard ran into the largest building to emerge a moment later accompanied by three other men. They all stood just outside the door, watching and waiting.

Biggles, with Marcel at his elbow, walked up. 'Where's Doctor Hara?' he enquired.

'The King is inside, resting,' answered one of the men, speaking with a strange accent.

'I'm sorry to disturb him but I want to talk to him,' said Biggles, curtly. 'And don't give me this King nonsense. I haven't come here to play games.'

'This is no game, as you'll find out,' said the man, glaring at Biggles with cold hostility. 'You can't give orders to the King.'

'What are you – the Prime Minister?'

'Yes.'

Biggles flickered a smile at Marcel. 'It looks as if, like Alice, we've dropped into Wonderland.' He turned back to the spokesman of the party. 'Would your name by any chance be Ronbach?'

'It would.'

'What office did Swenson fill?'

'Minister of Works.'

'Well, you'd better see about appointing a new one.'

'What do you mean by that?'

'Swenson's met with an accident. I doubt if he'll be coming back.'

'Where is he?'

'The last I saw of him he was going backwards over a ravine. Your two "guards" know the place. But that's enough of this nonsense. Tell Hara to lay off this pantomime stuff for a little while and we may come to terms.'

After a brief hesitation the man went into the building, but was back within a minute. 'The King will see you,' he announced.

'That's very kind of him,' acknowledged Biggles, with biting sarcasm.

With Marcel keeping close he followed the man into the building.

There was not much of a King's palace about the room in which they found themselves. The walls were whitewashed and as bare of decoration as those of a hospital ward. At the far end there was a low dais on which had been mounted, in the manner of a throne, a large gilded chair. There was a less important chair on either side. In front of the chairs was a bench, strewn with papers. There was an inkstand and a lamp among other odds and ends. On the throne, dressed in a white garment in the style of a bath robe, was the self-appointed King of Oratovoa.

He was a big man of between fifty and sixty years of age, clean shaven, with a high dome of a forehead even allowing for frontal baldness. His face was large and square and fell into heavy lines. The nose was prominent. Dark glasses, horn-rimmed, concealed his eyes. Taken altogether it was a strong face.

In dead silence Biggles walked right up to the dais, pulled down the two empty chairs, sat in one and offered the other to Marcel. 'I'm sure you won't mind, but I've just had a long walk and I'm rather tired,' he said, casually.

Ronbach and his companions, recovering from their surprise at this presumption, strode forward as if to do something about it; but the King raised a hand and they stopped.

Looking at Biggles, in a deep hard voice he asked: 'Who are you and what do you want?'

Biggles answered. 'I'll tell you, and if you can't be civil I'd advise you not to be rude. My name is Bigglesworth. Briefly, as a representative of the British Government I was sent here in the first place to warn anyone resident on the island that, as it comes within possible range of nuclear tests, there may be a danger of radioactive contamination.'

'Then take your infernal tests somewhere else,' shouted the self-styled King.

'I haven't finished yet,' went on Biggles, imperturbably. 'I have told you what was my duty in the first place. That now becomes secondary. Since I arrived here I have received information that a number of people, of several nationalities, are being detained here against their will.'

'Who told you that?'

'Who told me is of no importance.'

'Do you believe it?'

'I do.'

'What are you going to do about it?'

'That, to some extent, depends on you. One thing is certain. You can't go on with this. What exactly are you doing here?'

'So you want to know what I am doing?'

'Yes.'

'And if I refuse to tell you?'

'It will make little difference. I shall return home and report to my government certain facts that have already been brought to my notice, in which case, unless you have an acceptable explanation, you may find yourself facing some serious charges.'

'Such as?'

'Piracy, abduction, obtaining money under false pretences, and possibly murder. I could have returned home at once with this information but decided first to hear if you have an explanation to offer.'

'Would it interest you to know that I am engaged in an experiment which may be the salvation of the human race?'

'Not particularly. If the human race isn't capable of saving itself it will disappear like the great lizards that once dominated the earth. Nothing you could do will save it. Certainly not here. You may or may not have realised it but you've chosen to conduct your experiment on a volcano which may appear to be dead, but is, I suspect, very much alive. You may not mind that, but you can't force other people to share the risk.'

Hara's face remained expressionless. 'I have set myself a task and I shall proceed with it.'

'You will not be allowed to do anything of the sort.'

'Who'll stop me?'

'I shall. Or failing that, a force sent for the purpose.'

'Do you know what I am doing?'

'Yes. I asked you as a matter of courtesy.'

'How do you know?'

'I was given the information by one of your dupes.'

'What objection can the British Government have to my living here?'

'Oh really, Dr Hara, that's a ridiculous question and you know it. Other governments are involved. In the first place you brought people here by misrepresentation. You are keeping them here by force. You have seized a ship that doesn't belong to you, and you have introduced a pack of dogs that are a menace to anyone landing here. These animals have already been responsible for at least one death, to my certain knowledge. If you seriously believe that this sort of thing can be allowed to go on you must have a poor opinion of European administration.'

'I have.'

'In that case you will soon be disillusioned.'

'What are you going to do about it?'

'At this juncture I'm prepared to offer you terms which in the circumstances are more reasonable than you deserve. First, these dogs will have to be destroyed. Secondly, all the people who wish to leave the island must be allowed to do so. You, and those who wish to stay here, may do so pending a decision by my Government on your further occupation.'

'And if I refuse?'

'I shall return home and make my report, holding you responsible for anything that may happen here between now and the time you are ejected by force.'

'What makes you think you will be allowed to leave the island?'

'Whether I leave it or not will make no difference. If I fail to return home other people will soon be here to find out why. I'm trying to be reasonable in the hope of saving trouble for everyone. Neither threats nor force will help you.'

'We shall see about that.'

Biggles shrugged. 'Very well. Have it your way, but I warn you that your persistence in this crazy scheme will only make matters worse. Whatever you do, as far as this island is concerned your experiment is finished.'

The muscles of Hara's face tightened. 'Nothing is going to stand in the way of what I have set out to do.'

Biggles shook his head sadly. 'Dr Hara, I came to you direct because I always try the easy way first – I mean the easiest way for everyone. I trusted that you would be amenable to reason. Apparently I was wrong. I'm not looking for more trouble than is unavoidable, but if you want it the other way, that's how it will have to be. Do as I tell you and I will undertake to leave you here until your case can be dealt with by the proper authority in London.'

Hara's expression hardened. 'You must be mad to think you can dictate terms to me.'

'I shall think you're mad if you decline them.'

'So that's it! You think I'm mad?'

'I'll keep an open mind about that until I see how you behave.'

'Have you finished?'

'I have said all I have to say.'

That did it. Hara, who must have been holding

himself in hand, now lost control of himself and revealed himself to be the unbalanced fanatic Biggles had suspected. Leaping to his feet he broke into a torrent of abuse. He cursed Biggles for an interfering Britisher. He cursed the British Government and other governments in turn, including, somewhat surprisingly, his own.

'I'll tame you,' he shouted. 'I'll show you who's master here. Take them away! Take them away! Lock them up! Put a guard on them and shoot them if they give trouble. Those are my orders. Presently I'll decide what is to be done with them. Get them out of my sight.'

Hands were laid on Biggles and Marcel from behind, and on being turned they saw that during the conversation the room had quietly filled with guards. Marcel looked at Biggles with an expression that seemed to ask if he were prepared to submit to this treatment. Biggles merely shrugged, making it clear that at this juncture he was unwilling to resort to defensive measures which could only result in bloodshed and would probably end by them both being killed on the spot.

So they allowed themselves to be disarmed and led away to a nearby building which turned out to be a single room, and from its character was obviously intended for the confinement of unruly prisoners. The floor was bare earth. There was no furniture of any sort. A single barred window, unglazed, high up in the wall, let in some light. A door, a small, heavy affair that had once been a ship's bulkhead, was slammed and locked.

'*Tiens*! So we come unstuck,' observed Marcel, philosophically.

'I had to take the chance to find out what I wanted to know.'

'*Comment?*'

'This fellow Hara is as mad as a hatter.'

'But we knew that already, old cabbage.'

'We had only Alex's words for it. In court, hearsay evidence is regarded with suspicion. I wanted to see the man and judge for myself. You can't talk sense to a man who has a bug in his brain. The trouble is, Hara believes in what he's doing – or he's an astute liar.'

'And this is where we land ourselves.'

'I can't say I'm surprised. But the alternative to what I did, as I pointed out, was to go home with the job half done. To try to take the place by force and release the prisoners was not a practicable proposition. At home we should have been accused of starting a war. When Hara has had time to ponder the situation he may think better of the action he has taken. If he has any sanity left he'll realise that I told the truth when I said no matter what he does to us the lunatic game he's been playing here is finished. Those helping him must know that. Hara must have a powerful personality to keep them under his thumb.'

'He's a man to fear.'

'Definitely, although as a matter of fact I'm more afraid of the island itself than I am of him.'

'The island?'

'Oratovoa is boiling up for another eruption.'

'*Zut alors!* You really think that?'

'I'm so certain of it that I shall be glad to get off it. When I was talking to Hara I distinctly felt a tremor under my feet. Hara must have felt it, too, and from the fact that he ignored it I can only conclude that here it's such a common occurrence that no one pays any attention. It's not unusual for an apparently extinct volcano to blow its lid off. It may, or may not, give a few warning bumps. Apart from Krakatoa, which I've already mentioned, two thousand years ago people were living in the crater of Vesuvius when it suddenly coughed its innards out. The same with Mont Pelée, on the island of Martinique in the West Indies, at the beginning of the century. If an island of that size could wipe out nearly thirty thousand people in one bang, this thing we're standing on, when the mood comes on it, would make short work of everyone here. It might not happen for a long time, but it could happen tomorrow.'

'A charming thought to go to bed with,' said Marcel, pithily. 'What are we going to do?'

'That's an easy question to answer,' replied Biggles. 'Nothing. Or put it this way. All we can do is wait to see what Hara intends to do. In the meantime, Ginger may decide to do something. He'll have to be smart about it.'

'You're thinking of the plane?'

'Of course. Hara must know how we reached the island. No doubt he saw the aircraft when we flew over the crater. He'll guess it's still here, and there aren't many places where it could be. Unless he's a complete fool, and however crazy he may be I'm sure he isn't that, his next step will be to find it to prevent it from leaving.'

'Algy and Bertie will see that doesn't happen,' declared Marcel, confidently.

'I hope you're right,' said Biggles.

Chapter 10

UP TO GINGER

Ginger and Axel had found a more or less comfortable position just under the brow of the hill, so that they had only to raise themselves up to command a view of the open ground between them and the lip of the crater over which they had watched Biggles and Marcel disappear. There, in accordance with instructions, they settled down to wait.

For some time they were entertained by the stupendous view before them, and more than once Ginger remarked: 'It isn't true.' In fact, it was like nothing he had ever seen before. To the left a hideous black precipice fell sheer into the sea. For some reason – a reason later to be revealed – it was avoided by the clouds of seabirds. Sometimes they approached it, but, Ginger noticed, they never settled on it. Always at the last moment they wheeled away in a chorus of discordant cries.

On the right, ridged and split by ravines, the ground fell away at a steep angle into the forest belt far below. This was the slope up which they had travelled to the top of the mountain, although, looking down on it, Ginger found it hard to believe they had actually done what appeared to be impossible. The thought of the descent, should they be forced to return that way, filled him with something like dismay, although to be sure,

Sven was already on his way down. He had accepted the task without demur although he must have been aware of the risks involved. Even a twisted ankle on that treacherous slope, and that might easily happen, would be a serious matter. Ginger watched the open areas thinking he might see him, although in such a chaos of boulders, crags and pinnacles of rock, he hardly expected to do so. Nor, in fact, did he.

Immediately in front of them was the ravine into which Swenson had fallen, the bottom hidden under a tangle of tropical vegetation. Beyond it and below ran the green belt of jungle through which, unseen, ran what had become known as the dog track. Still further on and below, perhaps a mile away in a straight line, lay the ocean, its deep blue surface unbroken by a mark of any sort to catch the eye. Only the seaward end of the inlet could be seen, a narrow ribbon of water that disappeared behind the tops of the intervening forest trees. It was not possible, therefore, to see the aircraft, and after considering the matter for some time Ginger suggested to Axel that it might be a good thing to move their position to one which gave a better view of the inlet.

'If we can see the machine we should be able to see Sven arrive,' he said. 'It would be something to know he had got down all right. We should also know if Algy had to move.'

'Do you think he may have to move?'

'I don't know. But when Hara realises how vital the aircraft is to Biggles he may try to damage it to prevent him from leaving.'

They moved a little way along the slope and

presently found what they sought, a vantage point that overlooked the inner end of the anchorage, and, of course, the aircraft. To Ginger's satisfaction it was still in the same place.

All this time their greatest enemy was the sun. It struck down with rays of blistering heat which the porous rock absorbed and flung up again. Nothing could be done about it although from time to time they sought relief by crawling into any small patches of shade cast by boulders, and on one occasion by a long-dead fallen tree; but the respite was brief, for as the sun, now past its zenith, fell towards the sea, it found them again. Ginger, trying to forget the discomfort, occupied himself with whittling a heavy cudgel, thinking it might be useful against the dogs should they come into conflict with them.

The afternoon wore on to evening. They saw nothing of Sven. Nor did they see any movement on the flying-boat, from which Ginger could only suppose that Algy and Bertie had sought refuge from the intense heat inside the cabin.

At his invitation Axel told in more detail of events on the island since his arrival, and he was still so engaged when there occurred an incident which, not dangerous in itself, caused them to stare at each other before scrambling to their feet. The ground on which they were reclining quivered, as if it had been struck a blow with a great hammer. At the same time there came, from below them it seemed, a deep rumbling noise. The tremor lasted for three or four seconds. That this was not imagination was proved when several small pieces of the black cliff broke off and went crashing down into the void. Everywhere on the lower slopes the gulls left their perches and wheeled, screaming.

'My gosh!' cried Ginger, his face blanching. 'It's an earthquake.' He looked around desperately, and, as he quickly realised, foolishly, for a way of escape.

'That has happened three or four times since I came here,' stated Axel, calmly.

'The sooner I'm off this lump of jelly the happier I'll be,' declared Ginger, dry-lipped. 'It's terrifying. Now I know Hara is mad. No man in his right mind would stay here. No wonder the gulls don't sit on that cliff. It's falling apart. I heard stuff falling on the other side, too. The whole place is falling to pieces. I hope to goodness Biggles isn't going to be long. And what about Sven, amongst all those rocks. Look! Algy and Bertie must have felt something, or heard something. They've come out to see what it was.'

Two microscopic figures had appeared on the hull, staring up at the mountain. They stood there for a minute or two and then retired again into the cabin.

'You know, Axel, this puts a different complexion on this whole daft business,' asserted Ginger, seriously. 'I hope Biggles will realise it. This sitting on a million ton bomb that might explode at any moment isn't funny.'

'In the crater they may not have felt that tremor,' said Axel. 'The shocks seem to be local. Sometimes it's one side of the mountain, sometimes the other.'

'What a horror,' muttered Ginger. 'For the rest of the time I'm here I shall be waiting for it to happen again.'

'Hara says there's nothing to worry about.'

'Then as I said before, he must be nuts.'

'He says this has probably been going on for

hundreds of years and it may go on for hundreds more.'

'I only hope he's right,' said Ginger, shortly.

They resumed their seats, uneasily, fearing a repetition of the occurrence. However, this did not happen; but as the sun went down they took more frequent peeps over the ridge behind them to see if there was any sign of Biggles and Marcel.

Sundown brought a new discomfort in the shape of a sharp downpour of rain that soaked them to the skin. It was cold rain, too, and the shock of it after the heat set their teeth chattering.

'This happens regularly, nearly every evening,' said Axel. 'Tomorrow will be another day like today.'

'What a place,' muttered Ginger, disgustedly. 'What on earth can Biggles be doing?'

Axel did not answer.

Anxiety mounted as the sun sank into the empty ocean and darkness dropped from the sky to cover the island like a cloak. Biggles had allowed himself twenty-four hours, pondered Ginger, but, nevertheless, he could not help feeling that had his interview with Hara passed off smoothly he would have been back by now.

They passed an anxious, uncomfortable night, taking it in turns to keep watch for the return of Biggles and Marcel. Twice Ginger thought he felt a slight tremor pass through the ground on which he was lying, and this did nothing to ease his mind.

Dawn, in a blaze of colour, brought some slight relief, for as Ginger remarked in a disgruntled voice, they could at least see what they were doing, and the rocks had been given a chance to cool down. They could not see the aircraft because, as on the previous day, and presumably every day at that hour, the lower slopes of the mountain were shrouded in drifts of grey, opaque mist. Later, when these were dispersed by the rising sun they saw the machine at the same mooring, apparently unharmed; which, as Ginger remarked, was something to be thankful for. Occasionally a figure could be seen moving on the hull, and on one occasion Ginger saw two figures there together. They were too far off for recognition but he thought they were Algy and Bertie. What worried him was, he never saw three people there at the same time, as might have been expected had Sven got down safely. He did not mention his fears to Axel, who may have been thinking on the same lines.

They made a frugal breakfast from the remains of the food they had brought with them.

They continued to watch the ridge behind them, and the flying-boat, while the sun made its daily journey across the heavens, once more flaying the barren rocks with its merciless rays. The only incident to break the monotony of their vigil came just before noon, when shouts, whistles and animal noises in the ravine below indicated the presence of men and dogs.

'What do you think they're doing?' asked Axel. 'Are they on their way up here?'

'I doubt it. I'd say they're either looking for Swenson or trying to find the track by which Biggles and Marcel reached the top. Hara will know by now they didn't come up the regular track. He can't know anything about us. I may as well be frank, Axel,' went on Ginger. 'I'm getting alarmed. I feel sure that had Biggles been free to do so he'd have been here by now. I can't think of any reason why he should stay, willingly, as long as this.

Having made contact with this cock-eyed King he could have said in five minutes all there was to say. The time limit he gave us is nearly up, anyway.'

'You think Hara may have made him prisoner?'

'I'm afraid that's what has happened.'

'Suppose he and Marcel do not come back. What will you do?'

'I don't know,' answered Ginger, slowly. 'Biggles said in that event we should have to use our initiative. That's all very well, but it means a big decision. As I see it there are three things we can do. We can stay as we are, allowing Biggles some extra time. If he doesn't come that would simply leave us where we were and force us to take one of the alternatives. We can follow Sven down to the aircraft and leave Algy to decide whether to remain here or make for Australia. Or we can go on into the crater and find out what has happened there. If I do that I wouldn't advise you to come with me. No doubt you've already been posted as a deserter, in which case, if you were caught, you'd get it in the neck.'

'I shall stay with you, whatever you decide to do,' returned Axel, calmly.

'That's up to you. Tell me. You know this place. Assuming Biggles and Marcel are being held as prisoners what would Hara do with them?'

'I imagine he'd put them in the punishment cell. There's nowhere else.'

'What sort of place is this punishment cell?'

'It's just one room, standing by itself, used as a prison.'

'What's the place made of? Have you been in it?'

'Yes. It's a building standing by itself with an extra strong door made of old ship's timbers. There's one window, high up, with iron bars. You can't reach it because there's nothing to stand on. There's no furniture of any sort, not even a bed. The floor is just plain dirt.'

'What are the walls made of?'

'The same stuff as all the buildings. Home-made dry mud bricks. I've helped to make them. It's one of the regular tasks. First you collect lumps of lava. These are beaten to powder with crowbars and hammers. Then water is added until you have a thick paste. Dead grass is mixed with it to hold the stuff together. All you have to do then is beat the mixture into a mould and put it in the sun to dry.'

'What in some countries is called *adobe*.'

'That's right. The bricks are not as hard as the common clay bricks we use at home. You might call them soft, but here they serve their purpose. The roof is thatch. All the buildings here are constructed in this way. There are no other materials available.'

'It wouldn't be difficult to knock down such a place?' suggested Ginger.

'I wouldn't think so, although, of course, I've never tried.'

'A man inside with a good knife could cut his way out?'

'He wouldn't have a knife. Everything is taken away from a man when he is put in. He couldn't make a hole with his bare hands.'

'Just now you mentioned hammers and crowbars. Where are they kept?'

'In another building – the tool shed.'

'Is it far away?'

'No. It's close. All the buildings are close together.'

'Is the tool shed kept locked?'

'I don't know for certain but I wouldn't think so. People are always going to it.' Axel looked Ginger in the eyes. 'Are you thinking of knocking the prison down?'

Ginger grinned. 'I may have to. I was merely exploring the possibilities.'

'Someone would hear you. There are always guards about. The King's palace isn't far away.'

'I can't help that. You remember what Biggles said about Hara not knowing anything about us. He called it our trump card. I have a feeling we may have to play —'

Ginger sprang to his feet, aware that in the discussion he had relaxed his vigilance, as a figure came into sight, dragging itself wearily along the overheated rock a little way to their right. In a moment he saw who it was. With consternation in his voice he said: 'It's Sven! So he couldn't get down.'

They hurried to meet him.

'What happened?' asked Ginger, breathlessly.

Sven sank down, obviously in a state near exhaustion. His clothes were in a dreadful mess, torn and plastered with mud. He had lost his hat and his hair was dishevelled. With his chin unshaven and face speckled with *nono* bites he looked very different from the smart officer they had known on the way out.'

'Couldn't you find the way?' asked Ginger.

'It was no use,' answered Sven. 'The rock bridge over the ravine has gone. I saw it go in the earthquake. Another minute and I would have been on it. Give me a drink. I finished my water long ago.'

Ginger passed his bottle.

After he had taken a drink Sven went on: 'When I saw the bridge go I tried to find a way round the chasm. I must have walked miles. Several times I lost my bearings and had no idea of where I was in relation to the fiord. To make matters worse I could hear those infernal dogs in the forest not far below me. During the night I was nearly driven mad by insects. This morning I had another try at getting down but I seemed to be surrounded by precipices and at the finish I had to drag myself back up here. My shoes were falling to pieces, anyway. They weren't made for this sort of work. I'll tell you this. Now that bridge over the ravine has gone you won't get back the way we came.'

Ginger was silent. The shock of Sven's statement left him with nothing to say.

'Where's Biggles?' asked Sven, looking round.

'I wish I knew.'

'He hasn't come back?'

'No.'

'What do you make of that?'

'Hara's holding him prisoner or he would have been back by now.'

Sven nodded, mopping his face with the damp remains of his handkerchief. 'I was afraid of that. What are we going to do?'

'We were discussing that very question when I spotted you coming. What you've just told us settles the argument.'

'How?'

'It was a question of whether we went down to Algy,

or into the crater to find Biggles and Marcel. Now you tell me we can't get down the way we came up, that's out. I've no intention of getting myself mauled going down the dog track. That leaves one course open. I'm going into the crater to find out what has become of Biggles and Marcel. It went against the grain to push off, leaving them here, anyway. If we all get caught in the same trap it'll be up to Algy to fetch help from Australia. What I'm afraid of is, the island may not be here by the time he gets back. I have a feeling it's about due to blow up.'

'That will solve all our problems,' answered Sven. 'You've no idea of what has happeend to Biggles?'

'Not a clue.'

'Are you going into the crater now?'

'No. The time limit is up, but I don't think this is the moment to go. I shall wait for dark.'

'That would give me a chance to get my breath back,' said Sven.

'You mean – you're coming with me?'

'Of course.'

Ginger looked at Axel. 'What are you going to do?'

'I shall come with you. You'll need me to show you round. I know my way about. Without me you wouldn't know one building from another.'

'That's fine,' agreed Ginger. 'We'll wait for the moon to rise. If Biggles and Marcel aren't back by then we'll go ahead and find them.' His voice took on a harder tone. 'If this crooked monarch wants trouble he can have it.'

Chapter 11

BRISK WORK BY NIGHT

Darkness fell, and with it the usual heavy shower of rain – the excess water drawn up from the ocean by the sun during the heat of the day and dropped in the cool of the evening. There was still no sign of Biggles or Marcel.

Realising that it would be futile to try to do anything in the pitch darkness Ginger curbed his impatience and waited for moonrise. He was now quite certain that something serious had happened in the crater, and even if he could do nothing else, he would, he resolved, find out what it was. He gave Swenson's rifle to Axel, who had no weapon. Sven had a small automatic similar to his own. He hoped there would be no occasion to resort to firearms, but it was as well to be prepared, he told the others.

As soon as the moon had climbed out of the sea, with the cudgel he had made swinging in his left hand he invited Axel to lead the way into the settlement, taking the route best calculated to prevent them from being seen. The actual objective was, of course, the detention cell.

Axel had said he thought it unlikely that they would see anyone at that hour. The prisoners would have been locked in their dormitories, so any person moving about could be assumed to be a member of Hara's staff, most probably a guard. As far as he knew there were no sentries guarding the crater as a whole, this being unnecessary.

Ginger asked why was it unnecessary.

'In the first place who would be likely to come here?' answered Axel. 'Then again, even if a prisoner broke out he wouldn't get far without his shoes. All footgear is collected at night and taken away.'

'To where?'

'To another little hut, which is kept locked.'

'Hm. If they've taken Biggles' shoes it's going to be awkward.'

The little party moved on in silence.

Axel's opinion about sentries, or rather, the absence of any, turned out to be justified, and they reached a broad shadow just above the buildings without seeing a soul and without an alarm being raised. They sat down while Axel identified the several huts and houses, naming their purposes. Only one light showed, at a window of the palace.

Naturally, Ginger's interest concentrated on the detention cell, confident that if Biggles was still alive and well that was where he woud be. It seemed inconceivable, knowing how the rest of them were placed, that he would stay there voluntarily, even in the so-called palace as the guest of the King. Wherefore he decided to devote his attention to the prison, telling himself it should not take long to ascertain if Biggles and Marcel were there.

For a few minutes they sat in silence surveying the scene, Ginger keeping an eye on the opposite skyline where a pale glow, swiftly spreading, indicated the spot where the moon would climb above the rim of the crater and flood the place with light.

'We'd better get cracking before there's too much light,' he said at last. 'I think I have the layout fixed in my mind.'

'Wait,' breathed Axel. 'I see someone. Look! Walking towards the prison hut.'

They watched. A man, plain to see by reason of a light-coloured jacket, was walking towards the small isolated building that was their own objective. As he neared it a second figure detached itself from the shadow of the hut and walked slowly to meet him. He carried what appeared to be a rifle. This, as they met, he handed to the newcomer, and after a brief conversation walked on. The new arrival took up the position he occupied.

'That was the guard changing,' whispered Axel.

'It tells us all we need to know,' returned Ginger. 'If there's a guard on duty there must be somebody inside to guard.'

'It must be somebody important, too,' opined Axel. 'They don't usually bother with guards. A man inside can't get out. That fellow who has just come on duty is either sitting or standing by the door.'

'Where's the window,' asked Ginger.

'At the opposite end.'

'This is difficult,' put in Sven. 'You can't approach the door while that man is there.'

'I wouldn't attempt it,' replied Ginger. 'It simply means that we shall have to deal with him. There shouldn't be any great difficulty about that.'

'Do you mean you're going to kill him?'

'I hope that won't be necessary, but this is where we

have to get tough. Fiddling about won't get us anywhere. I haven't forgotten that these people are ready to commit murder when it suits them.'

'If that man shouts he'll raise the place,' stated Axel.

'We shall have to see he doesn't get a chance to shout.'

'What will you do – stalk him?'

'That's the only way to deal with him,' replied Ginger. 'Leave this to me. Now I'm here I'm going to see who's in the hut. It's a one man job. The more people the more noise. Watch me. When the coast is clear I'll make a signal by standing in the open and holding my hands above my head. When that happens join me as quickly as you can. Is that okay with you?'

'Are you sure I can't help?' queried Sven, anxiously.

'I'd rather tackle the job alone. We might get in each other's way. You know what they say about too many cooks. Stay here and keep your eyes open. If I make a mess of things you'll have to act as you think best.'

With that Ginger set off, taking a diagonal course both in order to keep in the shadow of the rising ground behind him and to put himself in a position to approach the objective from the rear end. The light was still on in Hara's quarters, otherwise the place might have been dead. Not a sound broke the silence, which meant that he had to proceed with the greatest caution, watching each step, for even a rolling stone would have made enough noise to attract the attention of the guard, assuming that he was doing his job properly. But knowing that even a minor alarm would be fatal to his mission he took no chances. Time, fortunately, was not important. As the guard had just been changed it seemed improbable that there would be another interruption for an hour or more.

Still, it was a breath-holding operation, particularly the last twenty yards or so, because, approaching from the rear of the hut, he could not see the guard, who, for all he knew, might have moved his position. Should the man decide to walk round the hut, they would meet face to face. However, in the event this did not happen. He paused under the window, a black square high up in the end gable, but no sound came from inside. Resisting a natural temptation to make his presence known to those within he went on.

Moving with no more noise than a cloud crossing the face of the moon he advanced step by step, tight against the wall, along the shadow cast by the hut. Reaching a point within a yard of the door end of the cell he held his breath and risked a peep. The guard, a dark-skinned man, was there, his back towards him, sitting on a heap of rubble, gazing straight ahead. The rifle lay across his knees. It was just what Ginger expected. From the man's attitude it was clear that he was bored, and probably considered his task to be a waste of time.

Ginger had already made up his mind what he was going to do. In fact, there was only one thing he could do. The man would have to be silenced before he could make a sound or his effort would have done more harm than good. He did not relish the business but there was no alternative. To threaten the man with his pistol, demanding silence, would, even if his order was obeyed, leave him with a prisoner on his hands to complicate what was already a sticky problem.

Taking the cudgel firmly in his right hand he crept

forward.

Whether the guard heard him, or was prompted by some primitive instinct for danger to look behind him, is a matter for surmise. At all events, he looked back over his shoulder, casually rather than otherwise, and, of course, saw Ginger. His lips fell apart with shock and he started to get up, dropping the rifle in his haste; but before he could utter a sound Ginger's cudgel came down, with a force that snapped it in two pieces, on his head. With a grunt he rolled over and lay still.

For a few seconds Ginger stood staring down at him, breathing heavily and trembling from reaction now that the distasteful job was done. How long the man would remain unconscious was a question; but he did not think for very long. A thick crop of hair must have protected his skull. With no means of trussing the man nothing could be done about that, anyway. The next thing was to bring the others down, he decided, so standing in the open he made the prearranged signal.

Returning to the unconscious guard, whom he dare not leave, he picked up the fallen rifle and leaned it against the wall well out of reach. His next move was to examine the door – not that there was much to examine. It was plain, heavy wood, its surface broken only by a keyhole. He had cherished a hope that the key might have been left in the lock, but in this respect his luck was out. It was, he told himself, too much to expect. Still hoping to find it he searched the guard. Again he failed. By the time he had done this Sven and Axel had arrived, panting with haste and excitement.

'The key isn't here,' he told them. 'I've been through the guard's pockets. He hasn't got it.'

'It will be with whoever is in charge of the guards, probably Ronbach,' said Axel. He looked at the face of the man on the ground. 'His name's Pedro. He's from Tahiti. I wouldn't worry if he never comes round. He's knocked me about more than once.'

'All right,' said Ginger, tersely. 'Let's not waste time. The next thing is to find out if Biggles is inside. Axel, you stand here and keep watch. Keep an eye on Pedro. There's his rifle against the wall. If he shows signs of coming round let me know. Tell him you'll knock his block off if he makes a squeak. This is no time to be lily-fingered. It's neck or nothing now. Come on, Sven.'

They hurried to the far end of the building, below the window.

'Give me a bunk up,' Ginger told Sven.

Sven, bending his back, obliged. Ginger clutched at the bars until his head was level with the opening. 'Are you there, Biggles?' he questioned crisply. 'It's me, Ginger.'

Biggles answered. 'Great work. Who's with you?'

'Sven and Axel.'

'Sven?'

'Yes. He came back. He couldn't get down. The bridge was gone.'

'What about the guard?'

'I've dealt with him. He's asleep, but he may come round.'

'What about the key?'

'We can't find it.'

'How are you going to get us out of here?'

'Knock a hole through the wall.'

'With what?'

'Tools. Axel knows where they're kept.'

'Suffering cats! That'll take time.'

'There's no other way short of shooting the lock out with rifle bullets.'

'That's no use. The gang would be here before you'd done it. Besides, you might hit us. Try the tools.'

'Okay.'

Ginger dropped to the ground and hastened back to Axel. Pedro, he was relieved to see, was still unconscious, but stertorous breathing suggested he might soon come round.

'Where are the tools kept?' he asked Axel.

'Over there. That's the tool shed.' Axel pointed to a hut some forty yards or so away.

Ginger and Sven strode towards it.

'If this is locked we're sunk,' muttered Ginger.

The door, to his great relief, was not even closed. Inside, he struck a match to investigate. Leaning against the walls were stacks of implements for use on the land. Both selected a heavy crowbar as the most suitable for their purpose. With these in their hands they hastened back to the rear of the cell and set about the work of demolition.

Ginger's first blow told him that the task was not as formidable as he had feared it might be. Had the building been of natural stone it would have been a very different matter, but the lava mortar of which the bricks were made was soft, friable stuff, and the heavy iron went into it as if it had been cheese. The soft character of the stuff provided another advantage. It yielded with much less noise than Ginger had feared.

Sven joined in the work and the iron bars rose and fell

in turn like twin battering rams.

Within five minutes they had driven a small hole right through the wall, and after that it was simply a matter of prising out enough bricks to enable those inside to get through. With dust sticking to the sweat on their faces they levered away, pausing once in a while to look around and listen. But the only sound came from Axel, who reported that Pedro looked like coming round at any moment.

'Stick the rifle in his face and tell him that if he makes one bleat it will be his last,' ordered Ginger, recklessly, and resumed his labour.

'Okay,' said Biggles presently, from within. 'I think that's enough.' His head and shoulders appeared. Catching him under the arms, one on each side, the others dragged him through the aperture. Marcel was treated in the same way.

'Phew!' breathed Biggles. 'What a game! Where's the guard?'

'Round by the front door.'

'Let's have a look.'

'What are you going to do with him?' Ginger wanted to know.

'What can we do? We'll push him inside and tell him he'll be shot if he comes out.'

Still half dazed, the frightened guard was pushed in through the hole and told to stay there.

'We'd better pull out while the going's good,' said Ginger, when this had been done.

'Pull out – where?' asked Biggles.

'Back to the boat.'

'And leave these poor wretches here at the mercy of

this lunatic doctor? We can't do that. Anyhow, with the bridge gone we can't go down that way, and I'd rather not run the gauntlet of those dogs if it can be avoided.'

Ginger shrugged. 'All right. Then what are we going to do? You tell me.'

'Listen,' said Biggles. 'Before long someone will come along to relieve the guard and discover what's happened. If we try to leave, Hara and his gang will have us on the run. Hara's off his rocker, anyway, and in his rage heaven only knows what he'd do to his helpless prisoners. There are women here as well as men, don't forget. At present we hold the advantage and I feel like hanging on to it. The five of us should be able to hold our own against this half-baked gang. What do you think, Marcel?'

'*Absolument.*'

'And what about you, Sven?'

'What you say will do for me. There are countrymen of mine here and I should be a nice one to desert them.'

'That's the spirit,' asserted Biggles.

'Okay,' said Ginger. 'What's the drill?'

Biggles thought for a moment. 'There are one or two possibilities. We could tackle Hara and his gang now, while they've no suspicion of anything wrong. Another idea would be to set free the prisoners, tell them what's cooking and all march out together.'

'March! They haven't any shoes.'

'We'll soon find them. All the prisoners need is a leader, and we can provide that.'

'Fair enough. Let's get on with it,' said Ginger.

'If there's any hold-up we're likely to arrive at the inlet to find Algy in the air on his way to Australia.'

'Just give me a minute to think,' requested Biggles. 'We don't want to go off at half cock.'

Silence fell.

The light in the palace went out.

Chapter 12

BIGGLES GETS BUSY

'Well?' asked Ginger impatiently, as the moon soared above the jagged crest of the mountain to flood the whole crater with pale blue light.

'The big snag we're up against is the dogs,' muttered Biggles. 'Were it not for those confounded brutes there would be nothing to prevent us from releasing the prisoners and marching them down to the inlet. The skipper of the *Dryad* must be here somewhere, if he's still alive. He could take the men off. He need only run as far as the Marquesas. We should be able to take the women in the aircraft.'

'Leaving Hara and his toughs to stew in their own juice.'

'They'd have no means of getting away. But those dogs worry me, I must admit. There are so many of them. I doubt if we could hold them off with the few weapons we have, and a limited supply of ammunition.'

'It looks as if we shall have to chance it if ever we're to get away,' opined Ginger.

Biggles looked at Axel. 'Do you happen to know if those dogs are penned up at night?'

Axel shook his head. 'I don't know. I imagine they're left to prowl about in case a prisoner should make a break in the dark. One thing is certain; the only way you could get to the inlet after dark would be by the path.

You couldn't get through the forest, and you'd break your neck on those rock slopes.'

'How many men has Hara at his command?'

'Certainly not more than ten, including Ronbach.'

'Where do these men sleep?'

'They live in what are called the barracks. I pointed the place out to Ginger. It's close against the palace. You can see the building from here. There it is.' Axel pointed to a long low structure.

'Let's go and give them a rattle,' suggested Marcel. 'We should catch them all in bed. There are no lights showing.'

'We couldn't shoot sleeping men,' protested Biggles. 'I'm all against starting a pitched battle, in which some people would certainly be killed.'

'I'd release the prisoners,' advised Sven. 'The whole party would make a strong force.'

'That would still leave us with the problem of getting through the dogs to the inlet. There are women to be considered, don't forget.'

'We shall have to get through those dogs whatever we do,' Ginger pointed out.

'Unless I can make Hara see sense,' returned Biggles.

'The man is *fou*,' declared Marcel. 'What is the use of trying to make an imbecile see sense?'

'You could only get down that path in daylight,' put in Axel. 'It means staying here till morning.'

'Could you find your way down in daylight?' enquired Biggles. 'We should look silly if we lost our way and got the whole party bogged down in the jungle.'

Axel said he thought he could find his way down. He knew the upper part quite well, from fetching the plantains.

'To deal with those dogs, what we need is more weapons,' said Biggles, thoughtfully.

'There are rifles in the barracks,' stated Axel.

'The owners of them are there, too,' replied Biggles. 'They'd object to us taking them, so we should come back to the thing I'm trying to avoid – a free fight.'

'Well, let's do something,' requested Ginger shortly. 'This standing here nattering isn't getting us anywhere.'

'It's all very well for you to say do something, but this business could have serious repercussions,' retorted Biggles. 'Several nationalities are involved, and if any of them are killed I shall have some explaining to do. Give me a minute to think.' He staggered – in fact, they all did – as the ground under their feet seemed to move slightly.

'Don't think too long, old cabbage,' requested Marcel, anxiously. 'Let us get on some ground that keeps still.'

Biggles made up his mind suddenly. 'We shall have to split up,' he decided. 'Marcel, you and Sven go and get the prisoners out. Between you, you can speak to them all in one language or another. Axel can go with you to show you where they live. Take the two rifles and those crowbars and bash the doors open. Do the same with the shed where the shoes are kept. Having got the whole party out and into their shoes march them over the rim of the crater to the beginning of the dog track. Wait for me there. If I'm not with you by daylight try to get down on your own. Let everyone carry a weapon, if it's only a stick. If the dogs come for you, shout. Make as much noise as you can. That may help.'

'What about you?' asked Marcel.

'I shall take Ginger with me and deal with things here. By the way, Axel, how many people actually sleep in the palace?'

'Four. Besides Hara and Ronbach there's the cook and a house servant. I believe Hara brought them with him when he first came here. There's always a sentry at the front door.'

'All right,' said Biggles, in a tone of finality. 'Marcel, Sven, get on with your job. I'll see you're not disturbed.'

Marcel and Sven departed, Axel leading the way.

'We'll have a look at the barracks, first,' Biggles told Ginger, walking towards them.

'What exactly are you going to do?'

'That will depend on what we find and what happens.'

'Don't forget the sentry in front of the palace.'

'I won't.'

They moved on, taking all possible precautions, although this really meant no more than keeping in the shadows cast by intervening huts and pausing from time to time to listen. They saw nobody, heard nothing, and so in a few minutes found themselves close against the wall of the long building which Axel had said housed the guards. It was constructed of the same primitive materials as the detention cell, as they had been led to expect. The rear wall was blank, with neither doors nor windows. Seen in the brilliant moonlight from the front there was a door in the middle with small windows at intervals on either side. The door was closed. There was no guard.

Biggles walked on to the door and laid a finger on his lips. He turned the handle and exerted a slight pressure. The door opened. He closed it again, having ascertained that it wasn't locked.

Looking at Ginger he breathed: 'I wonder if the key is on the inside?' He opened the door again, a little wider. They listened. From inside came the heavy regular breathing of sleeping men. Biggles inserted a hand, reaching for the inside of the lock, and withdrew it holding a key. Again he closed the door, and putting in the key outside, locked it. This made a slight scraping sound, but apparently it passed unheard.

'They're sort of careless,' murmured Ginger.

'People get like that when they think they have nothing to fear.'

'Okay. Now what?'

'Let's see what we can make of the palace. If we can handle things without a flare-up so much the better. Come on. Watch your step.'

Biggles went on, making for the side of the building he had named. It covered more ground than any of the others, but here he had the advantage of having been inside. It was in the first room that he had had his conversation with Hara. Reaching the wall, after another short pause to look about them they turned along it to the front.

Arriving at the angle Biggles dropped on his knees and took a quick peep round the corner. Withdrawing, he stood up, and cupping his hands round his mouth, whispered: 'There's a sentry. He's sitting on the door-step. His rifle's leaning against the wall. This should be easy. You stand fast. I'll —'

At this moment the silence that hung over the settlement was broken by a sound so loud that Ginger's heart jumped into his mouth, as the saying is. It was, in fact, a resounding crash, and it didn't take him long to realise what had caused it. It was the door of the prisoners' quarters being burst open.

At first he took this interruption to be in the nature of a disaster, for the sentry must have heard it and would certainly wonder what was happening. As things turned out it may have served a useful purpose, for the sentry took a few paces forward, and although this brought him into view his attention was concentrated on the direction from which the noise had come. The fact that he had not bothered to pick up his rifle suggested that he did not consider the incident of particular importance. The trouble would come when he turned to return to his post, for then he could not fail to see them.

Biggles did not wait for this to happen. Stepping as softly as a cat he approached the man swiftly from behind, and pushing the muzzle of his pistol into his back, said softly, 'Don't move, brother.'

The sentry gave a mighty start, as he had every reason to. Very slowly he turned his head and looked back over his shoulder. He did not speak. Only his eyes opened wide in astonishment.

Biggles continued. 'If you want to go on living you'll do exactly as I tell you. Understand?'

'Sure. Sure,' stammered the man.

'Behave sensibly and you'll come to no harm,' promised Biggles. 'Who's inside?'

'King Hara.'

'Who else?'

'Cap'n Ronbach.'

'Who else?'

'Only the cook and the servant.'

'Does Ronbach sleep in the same room as Hara?'

'No.'

'Which is Ronbach's room?'

'Third on the right, after the audience room. Don't you shoot me, I ain't done nothing.'

Biggles lowered his pistol, and allowing the man to turn, looked hard at his face. 'Did you come here with Hara?' he questioned.

'That's right.'

'From America?'

'Sure.'

'Do you like it here?'

'No. I hate it wors'n hell. I wanna go back home.'

'Then why don't you?'

'I daren't tell the King that. He don't like that talk.'

'You behave yourself and you can go home.'

'What you want me to do?'

'All you have to do is stand still and keep your mouth shut.'

'Sure. I'll do that.'

Biggles turned to Ginger who, having collected the rifle from the wall, had joined him. 'If this chap here is telling the truth, and I'm pretty sure he is, it seems that some of Hara's gang are as fed up with the place as the prisoners, and I don't wonder at it. If—'

He broke off as from no great distance away came another resounding crash. It was followed by a confused murmur of voices.

'I imagine that was the door of the shoe shed,' said

Biggles.

'What a row they're making,' muttered Ginger. 'They'll raise the place. Why doesn't Marcel tell them to pipe down?'

'I've no doubt he has,' returned Biggles. 'It's no use telling an excited crowd to stop talking. But never mind that. You stay here with our friend. I don't think he'll give you any trouble.'

'I ain't giving no trouble,' declared the guard. 'I wanna go home. I reckon this place is gonna boil over pretty soon.'

'You're right, it is,' answered Biggles. He turned to Ginger. 'If a row starts in the barrack hut tell them to stay quiet. If anyone tries to force the door say you'll shoot the first man to come out.'

'Okay. What are you going to do?'

'Have a word with Hara.'

'Why bother with him?'

'I'm trying to avoid casualties and I must give him a last chance to pull out. If we take the *Dryad* he'll be stuck here with no means of getting away should the island blow up.'

'After the way he's behaved I wouldn't let that worry me,' replied Ginger, trenchantly.

'Wait here,' ordered Biggles.

He strode to the door of the palace. He was prepared to find it locked, but it was not. He opened it and went in. The audience room was in darkness, although enough moonlight came in through the window for him to see what he was doing. He remembered seeing an oil lamp on the bench in front of the 'throne'. He went up to it and lit it. Holding it aloft in his left hand he went on through the door at the far end of the room, behind the chairs.

He found himself in a corridor. There were doors along one side of it. He opened the first. A glance revealed a comfortably furnished sitting room. There was no one in it, so he closed the door and went on to the next. This brought a surprise. It was fitted out like a small hospital ward, even to what looked like an operating table under a skylight. Jars and bottles filled shelves that lined the walls. There were several cupboards. The air reeked of antiseptic. There was no one in the room so he wasted no time on it but passed on to the next door. This was the third, and, according to the guard, the room where Ronbach slept.

The man had not lied. The yellow light of the lamp showed a bedroom, with a man asleep in the bed. It was Ronbach, snoring gently. On a small table beside him stood a candle-stick with a piece of candle in it, a half empty bottle of rum, a tumbler, and a revolver. Biggles picked up the revolver and put it in his pocket. The slight sound he made in doing this caused Ronbach to open his eyes. Or it may have been the light. At all events, he woke up. For a moment he stared, then sprang to a sitting position.

'How did you get here?' he grunted, thickly.

From the speech, and the bottle, Biggles suspected the man was drunk. 'Get up,' he ordered, curtly.

Ronbach swung pyjama-clad legs over the side of the bed. His eyes went to the table, a hand reaching at the same time.

'I've got your gun,' said Biggles. 'I shan't hesitate to use it if I have any nonsense from you. On your feet.'

'What's the idea?'

'Take me to Hara. I want to talk to both of you.'

Half dazed with sleep, or drink, or both, Ronbach stood up, to sway unsteadily on his feet.

'Lead on,' ordered Biggles.

Ronbach's eyes narrowed. 'What are you after – the dough?'

'Are you talking about money?'

'Sure.'

'What money?'

'Hara's money.'

'You mean the money he took from the people here?'

'What else?'

'Where does he keep it?'

'In a box under his bed.' Ronbach's face registered what may have been intended to be a smile, but it was more like a leer. 'How about splitting it two ways, you and me, and pulling out of this dump together. Eh? What about it? I've had enough of it.'

Biggles' lips curled. 'Even for a crook you're a stinker,' he said icily. 'Hara will be interested in your idea.'

'You mean you're gonna tell him?'

'Probably. Don't argue. Get moving.'

'You dirty rat. I'd like to —'

'I know what you'd like to do. Take me to Hara.'

'Find him yourself.' Ronbach flopped back on the bed.

'Is he as drunk as you are?'

'Worse, I guess. He can't carry his licker.'

Biggles hesitated. This situation, finding both men the worse for drink, was something he had not expected.

He glanced at the inside of the door. The key was in the lock. 'You'd better stay here,' he told Ronbach. 'Try to get out and you'll get what's about due to you. I've men outside.'

Ronbach struck a listening attitude. 'What's that noise?'

'Your miserable prisoners have been let out.'

'Where are they going?'

'Home. You stay where you are.'

Biggles backed to the door, took the key from the lock, went out, closed the door behind him and locked it. He was not happy about leaving Ronbach, but in the circumstances, which were not those he had anticipated, he could think of no alternative. He went on to the next door. It opened easily to his touch. Hara was there, in bed, asleep.

Biggles put the lamp on the table and looked round for a weapon, sure that Hara would not be without one. He couldn't see one, but he knew it must be there, somewhere, probably within easy reach. His eyes went to the pillow under the man's head. Cautiously inserting a hand under it he found what he sought. It was a heavy automatic pistol. He put it in his pocket.

'Wake up, Hara, I want to talk to you,' he said, loudly.

Hara awoke with a start, stared for a moment wild-eyed and then groped under his pillow.

'It isn't there,' Biggles informed him, evenly. 'I've got it.'

'How did you get out?' shouted Hara, furiously.

'I have friends.'

'I should have shot you.'

'You've lost your chance.'

'What do you want?'

'A few words with you in the hope of making you see sense. I'm evacuating the camp, and —'

'You what!' Hara fairly screamed the words.

'You heard me. There's no need to get excited about it. I'm taking everybody away and I'm giving you the opportunity of leaving at the same time. When we've gone you'll have no means of getting away, in which case, should the island blow up, it's going to be too bad for anyone left on it.'

'Where's Ronbach?'

'In his room.'

'What's the fool doing?'

'I don't know, but it's my guess he's swilling more rum, trying to pull himself together. He's drunk. He's no friend of yours, anyway. Do you know what he had the brass face to suggest to me?'

Hara looked interested. 'What?'

'His bright idea was that we took the money you keep under your bed, split it two ways and went home together.'

Hara sprang up, mouthing. 'That — that —' he choked.

'Take it easy,' advised Biggles. 'Storming won't help you now. Your little kingdom is finished. All I want to know is, are you coming home with me?'

'I'll see you to the devil first.'

Biggles shrugged a shoulder. 'Okay, if that's how you want it. Speaking of the devil, if I know anything you're within two jumps of hell right now. That's what this island will be when it blows up. For the last time, are you coming with me?'

'No.'

'That's all I wanted to know.'

'You can't get down to the sea. My dogs will tear you to pieces.'

'My last job, as I go, will be to wipe them out.'

Hara's face was a picture of exasperation and fury.

'Don't say I didn't give you a chance,' concluded Biggles, backing towards the door. 'I'll leave you and Ronbach to cut each other to ribbons.' With that he went out, locking the door behind him and leaving Hara shouting incoherently.

Ronbach was hammering on his door. Biggles hammered back.

'Who's that?' shouted Ronbach.

'It's me,' answered Biggles. 'I thought you'd better know I told Hara your scheme for splitting the money. He doesn't seem too pleased about it.'

'You —'

Biggles walked on, smiling.

Leaving the building he found Ginger waiting, in casual conversation with the guard who seemed well content with the new state of affairs.

'The boys in the barracks haven't discovered yet that they're locked in,' Ginger told Biggles, grinning.

'That's fine. They'll find out soon enough.' He turned to the guard. 'What about you? Are you coming with us?'

'Sure.'

'Sensible man.'

'What have you done with Hara and Ronbach?' Ginger wanted to know.

'I've locked them in their rooms.'

'They'll get out.'

'I hope they will. But I think they'll stay put long enough for our purpose. I invited Hara to come with us, hoping of course that he'd do something about the dogs. But he wouldn't have it.'

'What about Ronbach?'

'He suggested that he and I looted Hara's money and divided it between us.'

'What a skunk!'

'That's too good a word for him. I told Hara about it, so when they do get free they're likely to be at each other's throats.'

'That's about the best thing that could happen. Pity you couldn't have got the box of money, all the same.'

'I'd plenty to do without cluttering myself up with money or anything else. By the way, I've collected two more guns, a revolver and an automatic,' went on Biggles. 'With what we have already we should be able to deal with the dogs. Let's move on, to see how Marcel and Sven are faring.'

The guard following, they started walking quickly up the hill to the rim of the crater, making for the place where a continuous murmur of conversation told them the prisoners had been assembled.

Ginger stared when they came into sight of them, perceiving that it was one thing to talk of numbers but another matter altogether to see them in reality.

'My gosh!' he exclaimed. 'What a mob. We'll never deal with them.'

'We shall have to,' returned Biggles, lightly. 'There can be no going back now.'

Chapter 13

BACK TO THE SEA

The buzz of voices died away as Biggles strode up. It was evident that the people realised the leader of the affair had arrived. Marcel, Sven and Axel, who had been standing a little apart, watching and waiting, came forward to meet him.

'Everything all right?' queried Biggles.

'All according to plan,' answered Marcel.

'Good. How many people are there altogether?'

'Twenty-four, including Sven, Axel and myself. Six women and eighteen men.'

'With the one I have with me that makes a total of twenty-nine for embarkation. I take it everyone wants to go?'

'They can't get away fast enough. I had a job to hold some of them back from going straight down to the sea.'

'Call out the owners of the *Dryad*. I must speak to them.'

The Dutch photographers came forward.

'You can see what I'm trying to do,' said Biggles. 'I want to get everyone off the island as quickly as possible. I can take the ladies and perhaps some of the men in my flying-boat. The rest, if you have no objection, will have to squeeze themselves into your yacht.'

The Dutchmen said they were only too willing, but one raised the question of food.

'I can let you have what canned stuff I have in my machine, and with that, and what remains on board, you'll have to manage,' replied Biggles. 'You haven't far to go. Make for Atuona, in the Marquesas. How long will it take you to get there?'

'With fair weather we should do it in two days.'

'You shouldn't starve to death in that time even with nothing to eat. Given time you could put some plantains on board and perhaps catch some fish. I should do the trip in just over an hour. If I can find a trading vessel in the islands I could send it to meet you. Failing that I might pick up some stores and drop them to you.'

That settled that. Biggles then said he would like to speak to everyone who understood English. Marcel and Sven could between them translate to those who did not.

The word went round and they clustered about him.

'Listen carefully, everybody,' he said. 'You're all anxious to get away from here. So am I. We have a problem to face, and that is how to get down to the sea together without injury to anyone or without anyone becoming lost on the way. We may have trouble with the dogs. You know all about them. The only way we shall succeed is by everyone doing exactly as he is told. The important thing is to keep close together. We shall travel as a column three abreast with the ladies in the middle. Two men armed with rifles will lead. Others, with small arms, will guard the flanks and the rear. Any dogs that attempt to attack us will have to be shot. That goes for the men who have charge of them, too, if they try to stop us. Whatever happens we shall press on.

There can be no question of going back once we've started. If anyone would like to back out now's the time. Is that clear?'

No one moved.

'Very well,' said Biggles. 'We shall start as soon as it's light enough to see what we're doing. Until then you can relax.'

He then chose the men who would carry firearms and allocated their positions. He told the married men to stay close to their wives for their protection. As many people as possible would arm themselves with sticks and stones as these became available. That was all. Most people sat down to wait for zero hour.

'We'd better keep watch on the crater in case any of the gang break out and try following us,' Biggles said quietly to Ginger. 'Let's have a look.'

Marcel went with them as they walked the short distance up the incline behind them to the nearest point that overlooked the central depression. By this time the moon was well down with the result that deep gloom was once more filling the crater. A certain amount of noise came from the settlement – banging and shouting. A single light glowed like a fallen star.

'That must be in Hara's bedroom. I left the lamp there,' observed Biggles.

'They seem to be on the move,' remarked Ginger.

'I didn't imagine it would take them long to break out once they realised we had gone,' answered Biggles. 'I told Hara we were going.'

'What do you think he'll do?'

'He'll probably muster all hands and organise a pursuit – or try to.'

'Why do you say try to?' asked Marcel.

'Because I have a feeling that some of the riff-raff down there won't be too keen on it. Some might even prefer to go home. Hara is a fanatic, but that doesn't mean they're all crazy. They should have the wit to realise that if they lose the *Dryad* they may be here for years, on a smouldering volcano.'

'They're having a spot of bother down there, anyhow,' said Ginger, as a gunshot rang out.

'There will certainly be trouble between Hara and Ronbach when they meet,' asserted Biggles. 'I played one against the other with that object. If they started fighting among themselves that would suit us fine.'

'I can see someone coming,' said Ginger, peering into the gloom. 'He's running.'

'There's someone running after him, too,' observed Marcel.

Another gunshot rang out and the leading figure fell.

'That's one of them out of it, anyway,' said Biggles, calmly.

'It isn't Hara; I can hear him shouting,' informed Ginger.

'I fancy he has plenty to shout about,' returned Biggles. He looked at the sky, and the moon, already half out of sight as it dropped below the opposite rim. 'We shouldn't have much longer to wait,' he added, cheerfully. 'Dawn must be well on the way.'

Waiting is always tedious, and to Ginger the next hour seemed much longer. The moon buried itself in the sea, and the darkness that precedes the first pale flush of daybreak made it impossible to see anything beyond a few yards. The little crowd of refugees, huddled together, with an occasional whisper of conversation, created an atmosphere of unreality.

But all things have an end, and at long last came the first sign of the daily miracle so impatiently awaited – the pale grey stain spreading upwards from the eternal ocean.

'That's it,' said Biggles. 'We should be able to negotiate the open ground to the point where the track enters the jungle. By that time the sun should be up.'

He walked back to the main party, and finding Axel asked him if he was sure he could find his way down the first part of the slope. Axel said he had been over the ground so often that he could do it with his eyes shut. It was getting lighter with every passing second, anyway.

'Fair enough,' said Biggles. He turned to the waiting throng. 'On your feet, everyone,' he ordered. 'Form up in a column of threes.' He called the two Dutchmen to him and handed them the rifles. 'You'll go with Axel and guard the head of the column. Don't set too fast a pace or we shall have people straggling. Don't hesitate to shoot if you meet any sort of opposition.'

The two men said they understood, and took up their positions.

Giving Ronbach's revolver and Hara's automatic to the two Frenchmen he told them he relied on them to deal with any trouble from the rear and prevent anyone from straggling. He and Ginger would be on one flank, Marcel and Sven on the other, ready to go forward or back as circumstances might require. Spare men would arm themselves with any sort of weapon they could find. The women were told not to leave the middle of the column.

As was to be expected it took some time to get the party into a good tight formation. 'One last word,' he said, when this had been achieved. 'If I give the order to shout, make as much noise as you can. That might help to scare the dogs should they come for us. All right. March!'

Ginger had had some strange adventures, but none more odd than this, he thought, as he took up a position a little way behind Biggles. To get out of a scrape was nothing new, but to organise a mass evacuation was a new experience. He smiled as he wondered vaguely what Algy and Bertie would think when the crowd arrived on the beach.

The passage of the bare slopes, which took about half an hour, was accomplished without incident. Good order was kept, although, to be sure, this offered no difficulty, for the sky was now ablaze with all the colours of a tropic sunrise, and Ginger could see, for the first time, the people who had looked for an island paradise but had found only a miserable existence under an eccentric dictator. They were a motley lot, black, white and every intermediate shade, the men mostly with beards, everyone in rags.

Reaching the upper, rather sparse, fringe of the jungle belt, a brief halt was called while Axel pointed out the route to Biggles. Not that there was much to see, for the track was hardly discernible, being for the most part trampled grass and weeds with occasional footmarks in the softer ground. However, Axel assured them it was enough. He was familiar with the path, at any rate as far as the point where he picked up his loads of plantains.

Ginger took this opportunity of trying to see the inlet, and, more particularly, the aircraft; but they were too low down, and either rising ground or forest trees intervened.

The passage through the jungle belt began, with the rank vegetation steadily increasing in density and strength of growth; but through it the path ran on, plainly to be seen. In fact, it would have been almost impossible to leave it. There were places where it became so narrow that the column of threes was squeezed to a double line. Afterwards, the head was halted to allow the others to catch up. Underfoot, the ground was becoming softer and more slippery, and falls were frequent. These were taken as a joke, for, no doubt at the prospect of an early release, everyone was in good humour. So far there had been no sight or sound of the dogs; nor had there been any sign of pursuit. This was encouraging, but Ginger had a suspicion that the worst was yet to come.

That he was right in this respect was demonstrated as they entered the region of the forest proper. The light was dim, but against that the undergrowth was thin, as they had discovered on the way up, affording a limited view on either side.

Somewhere, from not far away, came a shout. It was followed, within a matter of seconds, by the crash of a rifle at the head of the line. The column did not halt but everyone was now on the alert. There was no more talking, and anxious eyes were on the leafy aisles on either side.

Ginger saw several dogs coming. They did not slink, but charged direct. Several shots were fired.

'Shout!' yelled Biggles.

Everyone obeyed, with a result that was startling, to say the least of it. Some of the dogs slid to their haunches, apparently not knowing what to make of the noise. That must have applied to their handlers, for Ginger saw a man appear, to stop and stare. He snapped a long shot at him and had the satisfaction of seeing him dive for cover behind a tree. Actually, Ginger was more afraid of the men than he was of the dogs, for he was sure they would carry firearms, if only for their own protection against their animals, should they turn on them. Should they shoot at the column they could hardly fail to hit someone.

He tried to keep an eye on the tree, but found it almost impossible, for in spite of Biggles' shouts of 'Steady' the column had increased its pace with the result that there was a lot of stumbling and slipping. Moreover, he had to give his attention to an old hound that made a savage lunge at him. He shot it, but did not kill it, for it turned tail and raced away.

This had an unexpected result. Ginger, watching it go, saw a man run out from behind a tree, waving his arms as if to check its flight. The effect was to cause the animal, enraged perhaps by its wound, to fly at him. For this the man must have been unprepared, because before he could defend himself the dog had knocked him down and then began to worry him. What finally happened Ginger did not see, for so taken up was he by the event that he slipped and fell headlong.

By the time he was on his feet Biggles was standing by him, shooting at a dog that was rushing the column.

'Don't shoot unless you have to,' said Biggles, tersely.

'We're holding our own, but at this rate we shall run out of ammunition. I must try to steady the mob.' He ran forward.

Mob was the word, thought Ginger, for the party, instead of steadying its pace as Biggles implored, had broken into something like a run, as no doubt was natural enough in the circumstances. Speed was, of course, desirable, but it meant that the column was beginning to spread out, and once that happens, as he well knew, a retreat is likely to become a panic.

However, Biggles must have reached the head of the line and halted it, for the ranks began to close up again. There were not as many dogs as there had been for a number had been shot, and these were probably the boldest, for the survivors seemed more content to slink along the flanks, keeping pace with the column.

As far as Ginger knew no one had been hurt, although he had seen one dog, which had managed to get into the column, hanging on to a man's sleeve. It was disposed of by a powerfully built Marquesan who had seized it by the hind legs and hurled it against a tree.

The shooting was now sporadic and Ginger knew why. Everyone was running out of ammunition and reserving his last one or two shots for an emergency.

Panting and sweating profusely in the sticky heat, for the sun was now well up, the refugees pressed on. Ginger had no idea of how much further they had to go, for hemmed in as they were by giant trees vision was limited to a short distance; but he felt that they must have reached the lowest slopes. The dogs, he thought, finding this a different matter from attacking a lone man, were becoming fewer, and often standing still as if not knowing what to do. He saw nothing more of their handlers. He heard no shouts, or whistles. Perhaps the men, too, realising that the escapers were well armed, had had enough.

Suddenly the column closed up like a concertina, and walking forward to find out why, discovered that the leaders had reached an open glade, and Biggles had decided to call a halt to re-form. 'It would,' he said, 'give everyone a chance to get his breath. We should soon be able to see the inlet,' he added.

'I think we're through the dogs,' said Sven, coming up.

Biggles agreed. 'The worst should be over,' he opined. 'Let's push on.'

'Listen!' exclaimed Ginger, suddenly, looking at Biggles wide-eyed. There was no need to say more. The sound that now reached their ears spoke for itself. It was the swish and roar of aero engines being started.

'Maybe Algy has heard the din we made and is moving across to the beach to be ready for us,' said Ginger, hopefully.

'I hope you're right,' returned Biggles, grimly. 'We shall soon know.'

They did soon know. The column was restarted, and another quarter of an hour, in which time they passed the scene of their first encounter with the dogs, they arrived at the beach.

The *Dryad* was still there at her anchor, but the aircraft was not.

They still could not see the mooring where they had left it. With Marcel's help Ginger scrambled up a tree, which he judged would overlook the spot. It did. One glance was enough. He swung back to the ground.

'They've gone,' he said, helplessly.

'I allowed myself four days,' said Biggles, slowly. 'They must have had good reason to move. What could it have been?'

There was no answer.

Chapter 14

PROBLEMS FOR ALGY

Algy had not moved the Sunderland without a reason although the shore party would never have guessed what it was. It so happened that the move was made at a most unfortunate moment, but in that there was no choice.

After the departure of Biggles and the rest on their hazardous undertaking, Algy and Bertie had settled down to a regular routine, which consisted mostly of taking turns at watching the opposite shore. This they did with painstaking diligence, for always aware of how much the machine meant to all of them they were taking no chances of losing it. In their position they were not afraid of the dogs, but they were very much concerned with whoever was in charge of them. It was taken for granted that from these people they could expect only hostility.

Of what was happening on the mountain they had not the remotest idea. They often looked up at it, speculating on Biggles' chances of reaching the top and what would happen if he succeeded in getting there. Still keeping close watch on the far shore, although the sultry heat of the day soon drove them into the shade of the cabin, they prepared a meal, ate it without much appetite, and washed up.

Not a sound came from the rank mass of jungle and

forest opposite. No whistle, no call, no bark of a dog, to indicate the menace which they knew lurked in its sullen depths. This was all very boring but they did not relax their vigilance.

During Algy's next watch Bertie produced a hand-line from their miscellaneous equipment and announced his intention of doing a spot of fishing. This, he asserted, in answer to a question from Algy, was not merely to while away the time, but in the hope of providing a change of diet. All their stores were of course of the canned variety, and fresh food of any sort would be acceptable. Algy had vetoed the idea of going ashore to look for bananas.

Using a morsel of tinned bacon for a bait Bertie cast his hook overboard. Within a minute there came such a tug that he nearly went overboard himself. Recovering, for a few seconds he hung on, the line cutting into his fingers; then there was a snap as the line parted and he reeled backwards as the strain was suddenly relaxed.

He turned a startled face to Algy. 'Here! I say chaps! Did you see that?'

Algy was smiling broadly. 'Of course. What did you hook – the bottom?'

'If it was the bottom, old boy, the bottom must be alive. It felt more like a bally whale to me.'

'I haven't noticed any whales hereabouts.' Algy was still smiling.

'Well, it was something pretty enormous. Nearly took my fingers off.' Bertie examined his hand critically.

'Have you finished fishing?' enquired Algy.

'Finished! No jolly fear.'

'What are you going to do?'

'Try again, old boy, try again. If I can haul one of these lads out, there would be fish for breakfast for a week.'

'In this heat it should be pretty ripe by the end of a week. No matter. Go ahead. Only one thing I ask you. Don't bring a shark aboard – not even a baby.'

'Not me, laddie. I'm nothing for sharks,' declared Bertie. 'Wait till I fetch another hook. I'll give the blighters something to bite on this time.'

He disappeared below, presently to return with a large cod hook, which he tied directly to the line. 'Let 'em try chewing that,' he murmured, as he transfixed another piece of bacon and threw it overboard.

The result was practically the same. A brief pause. Another tug. He hung on for perhaps ten seconds when again the fish went away with the hook.

'Oh, dash it all, this is a bit thick,' he protested, gazing down into the deep blue depths as he drew in the broken line.

'I'd say not thick enough,' said Algy, laughing. 'If you go on at this rate you soon won't have any line left.'

'The trouble is, they're all too big,' decided Bertie, sadly. 'Either that or the big 'uns won't give the little 'uns a chance.'

'This is the first time I've heard a fisherman complain the fish are too big,' scoffed Algy.

'Then some of 'em should try fishing here, old boy. All I want is one little haddock.'

'Try a smaller hook and a tiny bait,' suggested Algy, trying to be helpful.

'That's an idea,' agreed Bertie. 'Do you know, my mouth is watering for fish and chips, after all this hard tack.' He turned to go below.

How this angling operation would have ended, had it continued, is a matter for surmise. But it did not continue. It was brought to an abrupt end by something that gave them a different problem to discuss.

The hull appeared to be struck a considerable blow from below.

Bertie looked at Algy 'Did you do that?'

'No.'

'Then it must be those bally fish trying to get aboard for more bacon.'

'Don't be a fool.'

'It must have been a fish. It hit us a fair wallop.'

'It was more of a pulsation than a blow – as if it had come right up from the bottom and was transmitted through the water. By gosh! Look at the water! What did I tell you?'

The water of the inlet was rocking, a heavy swell bouncing from one side to the other. This of course caused the aircraft to rock. Several big fish broke surface, one jumping clear so close that spray drenched the machine as it fell back.

But it was what was happening ashore that gave Algy a clue as to what had occurred. A long low rumble turned his eyes upwards. Crags were falling off the black cliff and crashing down into the forest. More terrifying still, a slim rock spire was swaying. Even as they watched it they saw it break off and fall. The air was full of gulls, screaming.

'It's an earthquake,' said Algy, his tone of voice and the colour of his face revealing how he felt about it.

'Well, what do you know about that?' breathed

Bertie. 'Earthquakes are no joke.'

'Are you telling me?' cried Algy

'Well, we seem to have stopped quaking.'

'Yes. But for how long?'

'What do you mean?'

'I'm no expert, but I believe earthquake shocks seldom come alone. From what I've read, when they start they run in a series.'

'Here, hold hard, old boy, you're putting the wind up me,' protested Bertie.

'I've more than a breeze up myself, and I don't mind admitting it,' declared Algy.

'What can we do?'

'Nothing, as far as I can see.'

'A few more bangs like that last one won't do the machine any good.'

'You're right. Designers don't make allowances for earthquakes hammering at the keel. But never mind us,' went on Algy, anxiously. 'What about Biggles? He must be somewhere up there in the middle of it. If he happened to be under one of those landslides he wouldn't have a hope.'

'Don't let's think about that.'

'We may have to.'

'And there's nothing we can do?'

'Not a thing. We shall just have to go on waiting and hope for the best.'

'Not much joy in that, laddie.'

'We didn't come here looking for joy, and having seen the abominable place I wouldn't expect to find any. The whole mountain must be rotten. You could see that from the way it fell to pieces when it shook. Imagine what a really bad shake would do. Just a minute. Let's see if we can spot anything.'

Algy went into the cabin and returned with the binoculars. With these, for some time, he scanned the open ground near the summit. 'Not a sign of 'em,' he announced, at last. 'Not a movement of any sort. Even the gulls seem to have pushed off to a healthier spot.'

'Jolly wise of them, I'd say. They must know the drill.'

After that they sat on the hull, listening, watching, waiting, until sundown. They were hoping, of course, for the return of the shore party, but when darkness closed in they knew there was then no chance of that until daylight again made travel possible. On all sides around them, except for the narrow gap where the inlet met the ocean, towered the great mass of the mountain, black and menacing. There were no more earthquake shocks, although they were in constant expectation of another. Conversation became desultory.

'Don't forget there are other people on this beastly place besides Biggles,' remarked Bertie, after a long silence.

'What about them?'

'How are they going to feel about living on a lump of rock that wobbles?'

'What would you do?'

'Make for the sea, old boy, hot foot. They must know the *Dryad* is here. Maybe they're on the way down now.'

'What about the dogs? Would they face those – in the dark?'

'I wouldn't care to try it myself,' admitted Bertie.

'They might wait for daylight, and then come down

in body.'

'Perhaps. But what's the use of guessing?'

'I'm a bit puzzled about those dogs,' went on Bertie, reflectively.

'In what way?'

'How are they fed? What do they eat – if you see what I mean?'

'They looked half starved to me.'

'That may be done deliberately, to make them savage,' opined Bertie. 'I was once joint master of a pack of hounds and I can tell you they took some feeding to keep them fit. Even if this lot was allowed to run wild I don't see how they could fend for themselves.'

'Marcel said something about guinea-pigs being plentiful on the islands.'

'By jove! They'd have to be plentiful, too, to keep this pack going.'

'You ought to be glad you're not a guinea-pig on Oratovoa.'

'I am, old boy. Believe you me, I am,' said Bertie, fervently.

After that the conversation lapsed, and a little later, watches having been arranged, they settled down for the night.

It passed without alarm, and the first streak of dawn again found them on the move, Bertie preparing the usual meagre breakfast and Algy scanning the mountain through the glasses for signs of the shore party. He saw nothing.

The day turned out to be a repetition of the last, with the exception that they became more and more alarmed about the non-return of the shore party. Most of the time was spent in vain surmise as to what Biggles could be doing.

'He must have expected to be away a fair while or he wouldn't have given us such a long time allowance before we were to take action,' Bertie pointed out.

'It doesn't follow that he reckoned on being away all that time,' argued Algy. 'He was making allowance for an emergency.'

'Then all I can say it looks as if one has arisen, old boy,' returned Bertie, philosophically. 'Anything could have happened on that beastly mountain. Usually I rather like mountains, but I never saw one I liked less than this – earthquakes thrown in, and all that sort of nastiness.'

'All we can do is wait,' said Algy, moodily.

The day died, and night once more settled over Mystery Island, which, as Algy remarked, was living up to its name. It was passed precisely as the previous one. Nothing happened. The island might have been devoid of a living creature.

The dawn came with its customary display of colour, but it brought no sign of the shore party. Breakfast was taken in gloomy silence, each aware of what the other was thinking. Had the shore expedition gone according to plan, Biggles, or one of them, would have been back by now. The only question now was what had happened? If a tragedy had occurred, how serious was it? As far as Algy was concerned he could see the time approaching when he would have to make his big decision: whether to obey orders and make for Australia, or try to track the shore party to ascertain the facts, good or bad.

It was shortly after breakfast that things started to happen to keep them busy and so dispel the morbid thoughts that occupied their minds.

They began with a shout that seemed to come from fairly high up in the forest on the far side of the inlet. This, of course, brought Algy and Bertie to the alert. More shouts followed, one answering the other, proving that at least two people were there. Then, suddenly broke out the furious barking of dogs.

'I don't like the sound of that,' stated Bertie, deadly serious for once. 'Those hounds are hunting something – or somebody.'

'Biggles. Who else could it be?'

'Hadn't we better do something?'

'If we go ashore we shall be hunted ourselves. That won't help anybody,' answered Algy, lugubriously. 'We'd better stay here ready to move fast in case Biggles arrives in a hurry. He'll expect to find us here.'

'Those dogs are coming down the hill,' said Bertie, staring at the almost solid wall of timber that covered the lower slopes. 'If those brutes are running on a scent, and that's what it sounds like to me, it can only mean that the quarry they're hunting is making for the sea – for this creek, in fact. If he has a fair lead on the dogs he must be getting pretty close, too.'

'Watch to see if he breaks cover,' said Algy, in a tense voice.

Two or three minutes passed. Then they saw a man scramble out of the jungle at the water's edge, waving his arms wildly.

'That isn't one of our party,' said Algy. 'No one with

Biggles has a mop of hair as fair as that.'

'He's looking at us. In fact, he's waving to us,' stated Bertie, urgently.

A hail reached their ears.

'We shall have to go across and pick him up or those dogs will have him,' decided Algy. 'It doesn't matter who he is. Cast off.' He dived for the control cabin.

'Buck up or we'll be too late,' shouted Bertie, as he cast off.

'Can you see who it is?' yelled Algy.

'No. It's impossible to tell. He looks all rags and mud.'

To get a clear picture of the scene it must be remembered that Biggles had taken the Sunderland to the widest part of the inlet, which was some distance below the beach on which they had landed to explore the path; and, of course, on the opposite side. The width at the point that had been selected for a mooring was about two hundred yards. The place at which the hunted man had shown himself was again some distance lower down. From the aircraft to the man, therefore, would have meant a long swim, for which reason, no doubt, Algy did not even contemplate it. There were other obvious reasons why the machine should be taken across.

As a matter of fact, by the time Bertie had cast off, and Algy had got the aircraft moving, the hunted man had entered the water, and the reason why he had done so became evident when two or three dogs appeared on the spot he had vacated. One actually jumped into the water in its determination to reach its prey.

Algy sent the aircraft surging across the placid water

at a speed that sent waves racing to the banks, cutting the engines only when he had enough way on the boat to take it to its objective. By that time Bertie had been into the cabin to fetch the rifle. He had to put it down, of course, to lend a hand to the swimmer as Algy brought the cabin door alongside. In a matter of seconds the man was inside, on the floor, gasping, in a pool of water. Bertie snatched up the rifle intending to shoot the pursuing dog, but switched his target when he saw a man taking aim at him with a revolver. Both weapons cracked together. The revolver bullet struck the hull within inches of Bertie's head. The result of the rifle shot was not known, for the man ducked, or fell, behind some scrub. As the aircraft retreated Bertie fired three more shots into the bushes behind which the man had disappeared, and the fact that there was no reply suggested either that the man was down or had retreated to a safer spot.

Algy took the machine straight across to the far side of the inlet, to put as much distance as possible, as quickly as possible, between him and the danger area. There he switched off, and leaving the aircraft floating loose, for there was neither wind nor current, he went into the cabin to find Bertie giving the rescued man a tot of brandy from the first-aid chest. The patient certainly looked as if he could do with a restorative, for he was emaciated, hollow-eyed, half naked, his body scratched and pitted with *nono* bites.

'Watch that other bank,' Algy told Bertie. 'They may have another crack at us. Shoot at anything that moves.' Turning to the man now sitting up on the floor, he said: 'Who are you and what are you doing here?'

'My name's Martin Larsson. I escaped from the village,' was the reply.

'Village! What village?'

'The village in the crater on top of the mountain.'

Algy stared. 'So that's it. Your name sounds Swedish.'

'I am Swedish.'

'One of two lads who joined a South Sea expedition?'

'Yes.'

'Where's your pal?'

'I left him up top. I had a chance to make a break and took it. I was going back for him if I could find a boat or make a raft.'

'And you've been on the run ever since?'

'Yes.'

'Living on what?'

'Shellfish, bananas and coconuts mostly. I kept to the far end of the island. But I saw a plane and thought it had come down, so I started looking for it. That meant coming close to the dogs, and unluckily they picked up my scent just about the time I saw you. I made for the water intending to swim. Thank God you saw me. Thank you.'

'What do you mean when you say you escaped? Are there prisoners in the village?'

'Everyone is a prisoner except those who work for the King.'

Algy blinked. 'King. What King are you talking about?'

'The King of the island.'

'A Polynesian?'

'No. An American.'

Bertie spoke from the door. 'Well, blow me down! King, eh. That's a fair corker. Does he wear a crown, and all that?'

'Yes.'

'Chase me round the gasworks!' exclaimed Bertie. 'What next!'

Algy stepped in again. 'We've a party ashore. Have you seen anything of them?'

'No. I haven't seen anybody.'

This enlightening conversation, excusable in the circumstances, might have gone on for some time longer had not there been an interruption. A shot rang out somewhere up the mountainside. Others followed. Then came such a pandemonium of shouting that Algy and Bertie could only stare at each other in open-eyed astonishment.

Bertie was the first to speak. 'That sounds more like Biggles.'

'If it is then he's collected an army somewhere,' snapped Algy. 'It sounds more like a soccer match with someone kicking a goal. We'd better get back to our mooring in case we're needed. Give this lad some grub to go on with while I'm taxiing back to base.'

So saying, Algy went forward to the control cabin, and having started the engines began to work his way forward up the inlet; but he had not gone more than half way when there came from below a bump of such violence that it set the machine rocking and threw it off its course. He recovered instantly, only to have the control column almost snatched from his hands by another bump even more severe than the first. And that was not all. The water in the inlet seemed to tilt to one side, piling up against the bank and then recoiling with a force that nearly lifted the machine into the air. At the same time, from somewhere high above came a series of explosions that almost drowned the noise of the engines.

Bertie appeared, screwing his monocle in his eye. 'Here, I say, old boy, what the deuce is happening?' he asked.

'I'd say this is it,' answered Algy, grimly. 'This is a volcano and it's going to erupt.'

'What an absolute stinker, to do it now,' muttered Bertie, disgustedly.

The nature of air pilotage demands that the man at the controls of an aircraft must keep his head at all times. He must be able to think fast and act swiftly in an emergency. The exercise of this faculty is now rarely called for; but the unexpected can, and does, sometimes arise, and when it does a pilot's actions must be instantaneous. There may not be time for consideration. It may not be too much to say there are moments when a pilot acts without thinking. His action is dictated more by intuition.

The trouble with Algy was, the situation in which he now found himself was outside not only his experience but beyond anything he had ever imagined. No amount of foresight can make allowances for an earthquake. With only himself to consider he would have taken the machine straight off the water, or tried to do so, for that he would be able to do this was by no means a foregone conclusion. The normally tranquil water was now in a turmoil. Fish, some of them huge, were leaping high and the air was full of screaming gulls. Collision with any of them might do irreparable damage.

He was thinking about Biggles and the rest of the shore party. He was not to know that almost the entire population of the island had arrived on the beach, for this, being behind the headland, was hidden from his view, although it was not much more than a hundred yards away. All he could see through a cloud of spray was the stern of the anchored *Dryad*, bucking viciously in a confused area of turbulence. He realised of course that there had been an earthquake of considerable severity, but there was no reason for supposing that it would persist. The worst might already be over. On the other hand, for all he knew this might only be the beginning of something more devastating. Wherefore he found it difficult to make up his mind whether to stay on the water and hope for the best or take off in an endeavour to save the machine. With so little room to manoeuvre there was every possibility of it being thrown against one bank or the other with tragic results to a wing tip if nothing worse.

Bertie offered no advice, wisely leaving the decision to the man at the stick.

Algy perceived that if ever he was to get off it would have to be now, for a fine dust was beginning to fall, and even more alarming, grey stuff like pumice-stone was floating up from the bottom of the inlet to join a number of dead fish that had also appeared. He resolved, therefore, to try to get off, and from the air watch events. Should conditions return to normal he would land again. Should the shocks become worse, if he stayed where he was he would lose the machine anyway, he reasoned.

The decision made, with short steep waves hitting the side of the hull like pistol shots, he began a wide turn to bring the machine in line with the inlet for the longest possible run.

Chapter 15

ORATOVOA HAS THE LAST WORD

Ginger, on the beach, with a wider view, could see much more than Algy and Bertie in the Sunderland, where the general picture was restricted by the wings and other parts of the machine. On the other hand, one thing that Ginger could not see was the aircraft. He could hear it, but had no idea what it was doing.

Actually, he was finding it difficult to think. He was dazed by the suddenness of the calamity, for what was going on looked like the end of the world. The ground on which he stood quivered, and sometimes jerked; over and over again it seemed to reel under the blows of a gigantic hammer. The force was enough to lift him off his feet an inch or more. More than once he only saved himself from falling by dropping to his knees.

The mountain itself was a place of noise and confusion. He could hear the thundering roar of land-slides, but apart from that, what was happening he could only guess, for the air was full of sulphurous smoke and gritty dust. Occasionally there was a tremendous explosion. Fear of the awful power that was causing this tied his tongue. But perhaps his dominant sensation was one of utter helplessness. He realised only too well that the volcano, said to be dead, was in eruption, and that the giant cone, already rotten, was falling to pieces. There was nothing he could do. He knew there was nothing Biggles could do. In fact, there was nothing anyone could do. They were at the mercy of a monster far beyond human control.

The party had been on the beach for some minutes when the horror began.

When they had first heard the Sunderland's engines it was, of course, when Algy was engaged in the rescue of the fugitive Swede, Axel's friend, Martin. Biggles was not to know anything about that. He merely wondered, naturally, what Algy was doing. The irony of the business was, had the party arrived on the beach a few minutes earlier they would have seen the Sunderland leave its mooring. As it was, by the time they had finished their wild rush down the hill the aircraft had moved out of sight.

The surviving dogs, for some unaccountable reason, had all suddenly disappeared. Ginger wondered why. He could hear some of them barking in the distance as if they had gone off on another trail, but never for a moment did he associate this in any way with the behaviour of the aircraft. As for Axel's friend, he had forgotten all about him, assuming that he had died in the forest long ago.

However, the *Dryad* was still there, and Biggles' first step had been to call forward the owners to ask them to get aboard, start the engine, and bring the yacht as close as possible. This meant a short swim for the Dutchmen, but they raised no objection – not that there was any reason why they should, since they were as anxious as anybody to get away. So they set off, their Polynesian pilot going with them.

As Biggles remarked to Ginger, if they could get the

bulk of the crowd away it would clear the air somewhat. At this time, it should be said, Marcel and Sven were somewhere in the rear, watching the path in case Hara or any of his men arrived on the scene. The rest of the crowd, chattering with pardonable excitement, stood on the little beach watching the Dutchmen climb aboard their boat, obviously assuming that their escape from the island was now only a matter of time.

'We'll pack as many people into the yacht as she'll take,' Biggles told Ginger, above the buzz of conversation. 'They may run short of food but with distillation gear they should be all right for water. That's the main thing. The rest of us will have to wait for Algy. I can't imagine what he's doing but he shouldn't be long.'

'How can we be sure he's coming back?' questioned Ginger, dubiously.

'He's not likely to go off and leave us marooned here – not yet, anyway.'

'He must have had a good reason for moving.'

'I don't think it could have been anything very serious. He may only have gone to look at something. After all, he wasn't to know we had arrived here. Actually, in view of the dog menace, this is about the last place he'd expect to see us.'

It was at this moment that the first shock of the earthquake, that preceded the actual eruption, was felt. It was not particularly severe. There was a long low rumble and the ground on which they stood moved slightly, causing everyone to sway and clutch his neighbour for support. Curiously enough, the ex-prisoners did not appear to take this seriously, either because they were in high spirits or, from residence on the island, they had experienced the same thing before. Some of them even laughed, as if it were a joke. But Ginger didn't laugh. Neither, for that matter, did Biggles. Nor, obviously, did the gulls like what was happening. They took wing in clouds, wheeling and screaming. The dogs had fallen silent.

By this time one of the Dutchmen, with the Polynesian, was hauling in the *Dryad*'s anchor. The other had remained below. Puffs of oil smoke, aft, showed that the engine had been started.

It was now, with everyone watching the yacht, that the island indicated in no uncertain manner what was coming. From high above came a tremendous roar. At the same time the ground shook like a jelly, sending everyone reeling. Some fell. One of the women screamed. Looking up, Ginger saw a huge cloud of yellow smoke rising from the crater. Crossing the face of the sun it produced an unearthly twilight.

'What about Hara?' he muttered, in a voice that was not quite steady. 'If he is still in the crater he's had it.'

'I warned him this might happen,' returned Biggles, shortly. 'His common sense should have told him, anyway. It's more likely that he and his gang were coming down the hill after us. They had broken out of their quarters before we left the top. How bad this eruption is going to be is anybody's guess. The sooner we can get this crowd on the yacht, and away, the better.'

'I can still hear the Sunderland,' said Ginger. 'What on earth can Algy be doing? It sounds as if he's still on the inlet.'

'He isn't airborne – yet.'

'He won't go without us.'

'He may have to,' said Biggles, vehemently. 'Look at the water.'

'There was no need to explain what he meant. The water of the inlet, confined within its narrow limits, was eddying and heaving in a state of violent agitation. Fish were leaping in a frantic effort to escape from a scum that was rising in several places.

The yacht was now under way, the man at the wheel trying to back in. That he was having difficulty in handling the vessel was clear.

'He'll have her ashore if he isn't careful,' cried Ginger, his voice rising to near panic.

'He knows that as well as you do,' said Biggles, crisply, above the general uproar, for the volcano was booming almost continuously and the crash of falling rocks and cliffs was incessant.

The men on the yacht were now beckoning furiously.

'They daren't risk coming any closer in,' said Biggles. 'It means that people will have to go out to her.'

He turned to the crowd which, after the initial shock, had remained surprisingly quiet considering what was happening. 'They can't bring her any nearer,' he shouted. 'Those who want to go will have to swim out to her. There's nothing more I can do. Don't lose your heads. Help each other. It shouldn't be too difficult.'

No second invitation was necessary. There was a rush into the water, providing such a spectacle as Ginger never expected to see. Actually, the distance to the yacht was only a matter of thirty or forty yards according to how the surge of the water treated her, and of this distance it was possible to wade half way. Biggles did not attempt to control the throng, perceiving the futility of it. He allowed anyone to go who wanted to. All he did was shout: 'Help the women.'

'They'll swamp her,' predicted Ginger.

'I don't think so,' opined Biggles. 'She's a salt water craft, and if they can get out of the inlet to the open water they should be all right, assuming the sea is as calm as usual. The effect of the eruption may only be local.'

'Here comes Algy,' yelled Ginger, as the Sunderland came into view, making a wide turn.

'He looks as if he's lining up for a take-off,' said Biggles.

'He can't have seen us!'

'I don't think he has,' agreed Biggles. 'Ah, now he has,' he went on, as the flying-boat, instead of continuing its turn, straightened out and stood towards the beach.

'He'd have done better to take off,' declared Ginger. 'If he brushes that headland, or the yacht, with a wing, we've all had it.'

'He wouldn't be likely to go without us,' stated Biggles, evenly.

'My gosh! I don't like the way she's rocking.'

'If we can get aboard it should help to steady her,' said Biggles, shaking a hot cinder from the back of his hand.

It was beginning to rain cinders. Some hissed as they fell in the sea.

'There goes the yacht, anyway,' observed Biggles, with satisfaction in his voice, as the craft, rather low in the water with the load it had on board, backed away towards the middle of the fairway. 'How many are there of us left?' He looked round, counting. 'Ten,' he said. 'Counting Axel and the girl as half each, for weight, call it nine.'

They had hardly noticed the girl, a young Polynesian, for she was sitting on the ground with her face in her hands, apparently prepared to accept, with fatalism, anything that might happen. Ginger helped her up, to be ready for embarkation when the moment arrived.

The Sunderland was now coming in, or rather, being washed in, broadside on, in spite of anything Algy could do. Bertie was making desperate signals from the open door, at some risk, it seemed, of being flung out by the erratic movements of the aircraft. There were no regular waves. In the narrow inlet there was hardly room for them to form. Rather did the water seem to boil up from the bottom.

'Get aboard,' ordered Biggles. 'Try linking hands.'

Bertie now facilitated matters by casting a line at them. It fell a little short. Biggles went into the water as far as it was necessary to reach it, and returning to the beach pulled and held it taut. This helped to hold the machine steady besides providing a handhold between the beach and the plane. Along this line the remaining members of the party made their way, Bertie lending a hand to each one as he or she arrived.

Ginger remained with Biggles until the last moment. Then he, too, dragged himself along the line to the aircraft. Biggles came last, shouting to Bertie to let go the rope as soon as he had dragged himself on to the lower deck. Bertie obeyed, with the result that the big flying-boat, spinning sickeningly in a succession of whirlpools, was dragged by the backwash to somewhere about the middle of the fairway. To keep the aircraft under control in such conditions, at all events while it had no speed on it, was obviously impossible, and Ginger could only hope that things would be different when it felt the full power of its engines. What alarmed him more than anything was the steady rain of cinders, some of them, the larger pieces, glowing hot; for there seemed a fair chance that these, falling on the plane surfaces, might set the machine on fire. In fact, the spasmodic movements of the machine disposed of this peril by throwing off the cinders before they could do any harm. The slipstream of the airscrews helped, of course, and the faster the machine moved so did the risk of fire diminish.

There was a dramatic incident at the last moment.

Biggles had gone forward to join Algy in the control cabin. Most of the others, finding it difficult to keep on their feet, were either lying flat or holding on to anything within reach. Ginger, in the same predicament, had braced himself against a side window, staring with fascinated horror at the summit of the volcano. It was no longer smoking steadily as it might have been from an ordinary fire. Instead, every few seconds it gave a tremendous puff as though a mighty bellows was in operation, sending high not only smoke but clouds of solid matter. Along the rim of the crater had appeared a glowing crimson line that moved forward, slowly, but with implacable deliberation.

Something called his attention to the beach they had just left. It may have been a movement. He saw a man arrive, running. He carried a box, or a case of some sort.

A second man arrived. The one with the box dropped it and they began to fight. Other men came running down the path.

Through the haze of dust and smoke it was not possible to identify the men, but Ginger knew they could only be members of Hara's gang. Hara himself may have been there. With visibility as it was he couldn't tell.

What to do about this Ginger did not know. His first reaction was to rush forward and tell Biggles what was happening in case he hadn't noticed the men. Then he realised there was nothing they could do about it. Every second was precious. To go back would be sheer suicide. Even if they did that they could not pick up more passengers without overloading the aircraft. There was, too, a risk of the machine being damaged in the inevitable rush to get aboard.

However, what Ginger might or might not have done was settled for him when the Sunderland, its engines roaring, was at last brought into line with the inlet and raced forward on its take-off run.

Speed now made it possible for the aircraft to be kept under control, particularly when it started to lift, but even so the next few seconds were a period of suspense never to be forgotten. The keel struck several obstructions in a series of bumps, but whether these were caused by dead fish or pieces of floating lava was a matter of guesswork. Then, with cinders hitting the hull like rifle shots the Sunderland was airborne.

Straight in front of them now, churning down the middle of the fairway, was the *Dryad*. Vaguely, for his brain was in a whirl from the speed of events and the horror of all that was happening, Ginger wondered if they would clear the mainmast; but he need not have worried; the machine, now climbing fast, passed over it with plenty of room to spare. There was not a soul on deck. He could only suppose that the passengers had gone below to get out of the fiery rain. Uppermost in his mind was the thought – we've done it. We're off. It was not easy to believe.

As the machine came round in a wide turn to take up its course for the Marquesas he saw the *Dryad* emerge from the murk at the point where the inlet met the sea. The island itself was hidden behind a pall of smoke and cinders, presenting a picture very different from the one that had greeted them on arrival. Even then it could hardly have been called beautiful. Now it was an inferno.

A voice spoke at his elbow. It was Bertie. 'I say, you know, old boy, that was a pretty close squeak – what?' he said soberly.

'Are you telling me?' returned Ginger, fervently.

'Funny we should arrive just in time for the fireworks.'

'I don't think funny is the right word.'

'I must say it's a bit of a shocker,' confessed Bertie.

Ginger went forward and spoke to Biggles. 'Did you see Hara's lot arrive on the beach a moment before you took off?'

Biggles looked up. 'No. I didn't see them. I had other things to keep me busy. I knew they must still be on the island, of course. That was their decision, not mine.'

'They wouldn't have a hope.'

'As you say, not a hope,' agreed Biggles. 'I warned

Hara what was likely to happen; but he wouldn't have it, so my conscience is clear on that score. But we'll talk about this when we get to Atuona.'

Ginger made his way back to the cabin.

Chapter 16

AFTERMATH

Rather less than two hours later the Sunderland touched down on Taa Huka Bay, Atuona, and that, for all practical purposes, was the end of the mission that had taken it so far from home waters. The mystery of Oratovoa had been solved, and there was no longer any chance of anyone on the island being injured by radioactive fall-out from atomic bomb tests – or anything else, for that matter. As Biggles put it, the island had committed suicide, and there was little chance of any form of life having survived.

Later in the day, having given the machine a thorough examination for superficial damage, and done some calculations regarding the fuel and oil remaining in the tanks, Biggles made a reconnaissance to check that the *Dryad* was having no trouble. Seeing the yacht well on its way he returned to spend the night ashore. The *Dryad* dropped anchor in the bay two days later.

The rest was merely a matter of routine, taking statements from the refugees, fixing them up with temporary clothes and arranging for the Europeans in the party to return to their homes; for, of course, they had no money. None was much the worse for the adventure. The Dutch people had their own yacht. When they sailed, Axel and Martin, still seeking adventure, went with them as deck hands. A trader, en route for Tahiti, gave the others a lift. Consular agents there would attend to their needs.

One unexpected piece of information came to light. It turned out that it was Martin who had taken the oars from the *Dryad*'s boats. Prowling about after his escape he had found an abandoned canoe, or one that had been washed ashore; whereupon he had resolved to fetch Axel so that they could leave the island together in an attempt to reach the Marquesas. Paddles were the problem for there were none in the canoe. Remembering the *Dryad* he had swum up the inlet and taken the oars. He was still engaged in cutting them down to a usable length for canoe work when he had seen the Sunderland arrive.

A surprise, and not a very welcome one, awaited Biggles at Fiji, where his first step had been to make a long signal to the Air Commodore telling him that he had found people on Oratovoa and had evacuated them. The island, a live volcano, was now in eruption.

He received a reply ordering him to remain where he was pending further instructions. These arrived a week later, and were explicit. As he was so near, with servicing facilities available, he was to return to Oratovoa and make a report on conditions there. This would save the expense of sending a ship of the Royal Navy to investigate.

'Well, blow me down!' exclaimed Bertie, when he was informed of this. 'Back to the land that really does rock and roll. Ha! That's a joke.'

'Who had this brainwave?' grumbled Algy. 'It's going to be years before the place is any use to anyone.'

'Are we expected to land?' enquired Ginger,

sarcastically.

'That,' answered Biggles, 'has been left to my discretion. If the volcano is still active I'm not likely to singe my eyebrows by going close to it.'

'But —'

'We've had our orders,' broke in Biggles. 'The fact is, I imagine, somebody, perhaps the United States embassy in London, wants to know what happened to Doctor Hara and his precious pals.'

'Let's hope the old fug-hole is still blowing off steam,' said Bertie, cheerfully.

His hope was not fulfilled, as was ascertained when the Sunderland arrived a few days later to make its reconnaissance. A faint smudge of smoke was still drifting from the crater, but it was evident that the actual eruption was over.

'Quiet as a lamb,' observed Biggles. 'I don't think those dogs will worry anybody any more.'

The whole face of the island had changed. It lay grey and apparently lifeless under a layer of ashes. Broad areas of scum were drifting away to sea from the lee side. The inlet hadn't altered very much, as could be observed when Biggles flew low over it.

'What are you going to do?' asked Algy, suspiciously.

'I was thinking of having a look at the beach.'

'That means landing.'

'I see no reason why we shouldn't. The surface looks clear.'

'Well, watch what you're doing.'

'I shall, believe me.'

Biggles made two trips up and down the narrow waterway. There was a lot of débris near the banks, but the main channel, now as black as ink, appeared to be clear, so very gently he put the Sunderland down, and taxiing on to as near the beach as possible, switched off.

An eerie silence fell. To their nostrils came the reek of sulphur. The débris turned out to be a mixture of pumice-stone and dead fish, which included a twenty-foot shark.

'That must have been the lad I hooked,' declared Bertie.

'If Marcel had come face to face with that beauty when he swam to the yacht he might have changed his mind about sharks,' said Algy.

Marcel admitted it.

'Inflate the dinghy, I'm going ashore,' ordered Biggles. 'I'll go alone if you don't mind. I have a feeling that what I find on the beach won't be pretty to look at.'

The collapsible dinghy was inflated, and watched by the others Biggles paddled to the beach, pushing his way through the rubbish that covered the water for the last few yards. Powdery dust rose from under his feet as he stepped ashore.

For some minutes he moved about examining objects on the ground. He picked up a square object, shook the dust off it, looked inside, closed it again and put it in the dinghy. He had a last look round and then returned to the aircraft.

'Well?' queried Algy.

'There are three dead bodies there,' reported Biggles. 'They're past identification. They're half buried in cinders, which I fancy were red hot when they fell. I doubt if they'd know anything about that. The probability is, they were choked to death by dust and fumes. The others may have gone into the water, or into the forest, in an attempt to escape. The result would be the same, anyway. I have a feeling that Ronbach shot Hara, or vice versa, when we were on the top waiting for daylight.'

'What's in that case?' asked Ginger.

'The one thing they'd naturally try to save when they realised the island was finished. I'll show you.'

Biggles threw back the lid. Inside, neatly packed in bundles held together by elastic bands, were wads of notes. Some were English currency, but there were others. The top layer had suffered a little from scorching.

Ginger whistled softly. 'How much is there?'

'I don't know and I don't care,' answered Biggles. 'You can amuse yourself counting it on the way home. This must be the cash Hara took from the people who fancied life on a desert island. No doubt they'll be delighted to have it back.'

'Not to say lucky,' murmured Algy. 'What do we do next?'

'We'll press on home right away,' decided Biggles. 'There's nothing to remain here for. I'd say there isn't a living creature left alive on the island – not even a *nono*. The gulls, having wings, probably made for a healthier spot. We might take the tip from them and do the same thing. Okay. Pack up and we'll get mobile.'

One last word. The true identity of the man who wanted to be a king was never definitely established, although some time afterwards it was learned, from enquiries in America, that a doctor of the same name had escaped from a criminal asylum and had never been recaptured. He had associated himself with the underworld, and from the fact that he was known to have a weakness for titles he might well have been the same man. Whether he had gone to Oratovoa simply to indulge in this whim, taking money from unsuspecting adventure-seekers to support his 'kingdom', or whether he really believed in his 'experiment', the creation of a new race of disease-free people, must always remain a matter for conjecture.

As Biggles remarked, the odd thing about it all was this: even if the aircraft had not gone to Mystery Island his end would have been the same, although in that case, of course, a lot of innocent people would have died with him.

Finally, the full story of the strange events on Oratovoa was never made public. One or two newspapers carried a brief paragraph to the effect that the volcano of Oratovoa, in the Pacific, was in eruption; but the rest, with more important things going on nearer home, did not consider as 'news' an island which few of their readers could have heard of, would not have known where to look for on the map, and about which, as Ginger put it, 'they couldn't care less'.

MORE KNIGHT BOOKS

CAPTAIN W. E. JOHNS

BIGGLES BREAKS THE SILENCE
BIGGLES MAKES ENDS MEET
BIGGLES FORMS A SYNDICATE
BIGGLES SEES TOO MUCH
BIGGLES WORKS IT OUT

More exciting adventures for the intrepid Biggles, re-issued after many years out of print.

CHRIS POWLING

MOG AND THE RECTIFIER

Mog is the greatest leader a gang ever had; Mog's hero is the Rectifier. Mog's plans to follow in the footsteps of this mysterious Robin Hood figure are continually thwarted by spoilt rich-kid Howard Bygrave and his sinister chauffeur Mr Skin. By chance they all get involved with the Rectifier's plans, and something that starts as a game suddenly becomes serious.

A tangle of crises develops and somehow the powerful, elusive figure of the Rectifier is behind it all . . .

KNIGHT BOOKS